FALSE IMAGES

Other volumes in the CARE series:
  Is Life Really Sacred? by Nigel M de S Cameron
  Schizophrenia: Voices in the Dark by Mary Moate
    and David Enoch

THE CARE SERIES

False Images

NIGEL WILLIAMS

Series Editor: Nigel M de S Cameron

KINGSWAY PUBLICATIONS
EASTBOURNE

First published 1991
Reprinted 1992

British Library Cataloguing in Publication Data

Williams, Nigel
    False images. — (The care series)
    I. Title   II. Series
    363.47

ISBN 0-86065-954-2

Printed in Great Britain for
KINGSWAY PUBLICATIONS LTD
1 St Anne's Road, Eastbourne, E. Sussex BN21 3UN by
Clays Ltd, St Ives plc
Typeset by Nuprint Ltd, Harpenden, Herts.

TO
all those parliamentarians, both
MPs and peers, who are trying to change
the law to make pornography less available
in our society

Contents

Acknowledgements

Pornography is not an easy subject to write about. The book would not actually have been written had I not been continually provoked and encouraged by the Series Editor, Nigel Cameron.

Many people have helped me over the last few years with insights and ideas that can be found in this book. It would be hard to find a more helpful team of people and a more fulfilling environment to work in than at CARE's offices in London. It is difficult to single out individuals but thanks are especially due to Lyndon, Charlie, Luke, Ian, Tricia, Jane and Janice.

Anna Grear, who has worked closely with CARE, deserves special mention as she first made me think more deeply about how to approach the issue of pornography in a truly biblical way. Chapters 1 and 4 of this book owe much to discussions with Anna and to her writing.

Practical and pastoral support has been readily forthcoming from those Christians close to me in my home fellowship—The Antioch Community in

London. Iain Archibald has been especially supportive throughout this project and made many helpful comments on the first draft.

Two women, however, have had the most influence on the book itself. My secretary, Lesley, undoubtedly has the biblical gift of interpretation: of my frenetic dictation and scrawled amendments! My wife, Heather, has put up with much throughout the writing period including moving house. She is for me what the true image of womanhood is all about—physical beauty combined with inner beauty in perfect harmony.

All these people have helped, but no doubt mistakes will remain and these are my sole responsibility.

Foreword

Pornography is on the increase. It shows itself in literature, in newspapers, in the visual media, even in telephone chat-lines and computer games. A 'flood' of pornography has become the authentic collective noun to describe its latter-day impact.

Yet it is not for want of restraining laws that the flood increases. Indeed it is surprising how varied, systematic, and extensive are the range of legal restraints which parliament has enacted at different times to combat pornography. In chapter 6 below, Nigel Williams has listed a positive multiplicity of such statutory provisions, drawn from a whole variety of Acts, all designed to prevent, or stem, the flood. Yet manifestly the flood is beating the barriers.

Some might argue that there is good cause for this overwhelming of the traditional barriers of restraint. They point out that, in Western societies at least, prevalent attitudes to sexual morality have undergone an immense liberalisation since Victorian times and earlier. The wider, freer publication of erotic and pornographic material is thus an inevitable, and acceptable, corollary to that liberalisation. It is the law, they would argue, which should be liberalised, not pornography penalised, because the law nowadays is out of step with society's more liberal attitudes. C. S.

Lewis encapsulated this approach (although he was, of course, no friend of pornography) in his critical essay on Sex in Literature:

> ...one of the causes which led to the abandonment of our older penal code was the fact that as juries grew more humane they simply refused to convict. The evidence showed beyond doubt that the famished girl in the dock had stolen a handkerchief. But they didn't want her to be hanged for that, so they returned a verdict of Not Guilty.

But is it really a mark of being more humane today, that one should generally wish to find pornographers Not Guilty when they fall foul of the law? Alas, the law as it now stands all too often makes that verdict inescapable. We are therefore greatly indebted to Nigel Williams for shattering the myth that the contemporary growth in pornography is simply a benign extension of the more open and positive discussion of sexual issues which graces our age. Far from being 'the famished girl in the dock' awaiting a humane emancipation, pornography emerges in this study as a cruel predatory cancer bent on exploiting and corrupting real freedom in the interest of profit-growth. It thus needs to be confronted and denounced fearlessly and clear-headedly. For the divine splendour of human sexuality comes through as clearly in Nigel Williams' writing, as the almost unimaginable horror of how pornographers corrupt that sexuality, above all in the case of children.

It is a paradox of our freer and more liberal age that some areas of law have been found to need strengthening, not dismantling, as society progresses. Legislation on race relations, and racist publications, is a case in point. *False Images* makes it clear beyond a peradventure that the law on obscenity is another area where more muscle, not greater relaxation, is urgently called for in our framework of law. Nigel Williams has powerfully strengthened the hands of those who are trying to cultivate that muscle.

MICHAEL ALISON M.P.

1

Sex Was God's Idea

Pornography is all about sex and money. The pornography business involves thousands of people, from the corner newsagent selling a few magazines to multi-million pound empires producing and distributing material worldwide. Pornography has gained a cloak of acceptance in our society because so many people are involved.

It is easy to become bogged down in questions like the definition of pornography. Some individuals will want to embroil us in debate about censorship and limitations on personal freedom. Psychologists will argue there is no proof pornography causes harm. Within our churches Christians will say there are more important issues, like the homeless in this country and the starving abroad. Others will fear that a campaign against pornography is a refuge for people who think sex is a dirty word and are harsh and condemning in their attitudes.

This book attempts to steer a clear course through the pornography minefield. There are issues which need to be addressed. Hard questions must be asked—and answered! But rather than addressing these questions head on, I want first to look at a more basic question: what is God's view of sex? If we start there, not only are we in a better place to identify material which offends the biblical standard, but we will improve our attitudes towards those involved in pornography, so that we can reach out to help them. We first need to celebrate what is good before dealing with what is bad.

The Bible is very honest about sexual relationships and the procreation of children. This book cannot address this topic at any length, but I would identify the following themes from the Bible:

(a) Sex cannot be separated from marriage— there is no place in God's plan for casual sexual relationships. Right from Genesis we are told that a man leaves his own family and joins together with a woman and they become one flesh (Genesis 2:24). The relationship involves commitment, love and caring. Sexual intercourse is no mere physical act, like washing hands or playing tennis together. It is a joyful giving of one man and one woman to each other with the security that both have made a lifelong commitment.

(b) Children are the natural (though not inevitable) consequence of a sexual relationship—the Bible presents a clear picture that one of the main reasons for getting married is to have children: 'Be fruitful and multiply' (Genesis 1:28). This encourages a responsible view of sexual intercourse. It is one of the wonders of creation that man and woman can reproduce themselves through an act in which minute sperm and ova come together.

(c) The sexual relationship is joyful—nowhere in Scripture is a negative view presented of sex within marriage. The Bible fully recognises the power of the sex drive. Paul suggests men should marry rather than 'burn' (1 Corinthians 7:9) and encourages marriage partners to have frequent sexual intercourse together.

The clear impression from reading the Bible is that sexual intercourse is one of the most precious gifts that God has given. Not everyone will be able to partake in that gift, but the Bible is not stuffy about sex; it is practical and wise.

The Bible's view of women

As well as the Bible's presentation of the sexual relationship we must also address the wider issue of how the Bible views physical beauty, especially that of women. Most pornography is concerned with the presentation of women as physically desirable creatures. The Bible recognises the beauty of women. Esther was a woman chosen by the Babylonian king because of her physical beauty. Samson was attracted to Delilah. Solomon sang the virtues of his lover. God intended women to be physically beautiful, not least because they were made in his image.

But God's image goes much beyond physical beauty. It conveys above all else individual dignity. Each of us was made as an individual to be respected in his or her own right. We all have some physical beauty. Even the most disabled and malformed children can convey beauty through the sparkle of their eyes or the winsomeness of their smile. But more than that, there is beauty in our spirits and characters. There is beauty in people using their intelligence to understand a difficult problem and speak about it. There is beauty in the use of hands to create a work of art or a tasty meal. There is beauty in the strength of character to overcome difficult circumstances, financial hardship, or physical limitations.

God's view of beauty embraces all these things. The exterior of our physical bodies conveys what is on the inside. Have you ever noticed the transformation in someone's appearance after they have dedicated their life to God, or some event of spiritual significance has taken place? I recall a girl at my school who came to know Christ. She was not one of the girls we boys talked about as being especially good looking. Indeed, she was thought to be somewhat boring and a bit of a swot. But when God came into her life her physical appearance changed. Her face lit up and her eyes sparkled. What had happened in her spirit could be seen in her body.

The opposite is also true. How sad it is to see someone whom we remember as being physically attractive worn down by inner emptiness. Just as illness can make us look physically less attractive, so problems inside ourselves filter to the surface. Slumped shoulders and dull eyes reveal inner problems. Even the most physically attractive person cannot hide inner turmoil. Nor is it possible to hide misuse of the body. Those who have succumbed to an addiction to alcohol or drugs, or those who have given their bodies to sexual licence, will reveal it in their physical appearance. Old prostitutes are not beautiful women.

This view of beauty is reflected in those verses in the apostle Peter's letter (1 Peter 3:3–4) about Christian women not adorning themselves with jewellery and fancy hairstyles but relying on the 'unfading beauty of a gentle and quiet spirit'. Physical beauty on its own is a transient quality. It is made more permanent by the inner change that ultimately only Christ can bring.

Communication on sexual topics

One of the ironies of Christian history is that although the Bible is quite explicit on sexual subjects the church has frequently failed to be. Often sex has been seen as an improper subject for discussion, something to be nudged and winked about rather than dealt with openly. It is right to have a proper concern for privacy and not talk about intimate personal sexual problems in a public way where the individuals are identifiable. But given the apostle Paul's approach to sexuality in his letters, it must be appropriate for the church to teach on this subject and to encourage a healthy openness on the general issue.

Some communication is vital because our world is full of negative sexual images. Pornography is a negative image of sex. The positive image presented in Scripture is not much use unless we are able to examine it, discuss it and consider with others what it means. Too many Christians discuss sex in furtive tones with acquaintances at conferences or events after the inevitable packed seminar on some sexual topic. In my view teaching on sexual relationships is best handled within the local church and the family, taking every advantage of good-quality literature, videos and speakers from outside.

For example, within my local fellowship the issue is dealt with in stages:

(1) Families are encouraged to broach the issue of sex education with their children in a natural way in the context of the home. This can start from simple questions like, 'Where did I come from?' at an early age, through to a thorough explanation of sexual topics perhaps at age ten or eleven. My wife and I found it a most rewarding experience to spend time with our oldest daughter at the age of ten, reading together a book about the physical, emotional and spiritual changes that might happen to her over the next few years. We gave plenty of opportunity for private conversations between mother and daughter, but I was glad to be involved as well so that she could be secure in talking on these topics with her father.

(2) Within the youth group the issue is tackled and an approach to relationships between the sexes established which discourages casual dating.

(3) We have courses for older members (eighteen-plus) which include topics like the nature of male and female sexuality, and an understanding of marriage. There are separate courses for singles and marrieds. The marrieds' courses include some sessions for men and women together and some sessions where the sexes meet separately. Talks are

followed by individual group discussions of the principles involved.

(4) Couples preparing for marriage are encouraged to build a relationship with another married couple where all the implications of becoming married can be discussed. This includes sexual questions and practical problems like what the physical relationship should involve before marriage and what the expectation should be afterwards.

(5) Married couples who have difficulties or questions are encouraged to talk these through with another couple whom they know well. Sexual relationships in marriage can become stale or unfulfilling for one or both partners. My wife and I have benefited greatly from discussing this kind of issue with another couple.

(6) The issue will arise from time to time in pastoral home groups in a general way. I have taken part in discussions on issues like masturbation, oral sex, and male and female differences in sexual response within the small group to which I belong. Such discussions are nearly always in the context of a single-sex group.

No system of communicating on sexual topics is perfect and this approach does demand a considerable amount of time and effort. The details are less important than the general principles:

(1) Openness in teaching about marriage and sexual relationship.

(2) Privacy about personal details which are best dealt with on a one-to-one or couple-to-couple basis.

(3) Addressing the issue from an early age.

19

Some readers may be perplexed by my emphasis on this issue in a book about pornography. I make no apology. Generally Christians are too quick to point out the failures in a worldly understanding of sexuality without appreciating our own failures. The sexual relationship is a wonderful gift from God which we need to cherish, encouraging each other to approach it in the right way. Men need to learn how to treat women with respect and be able to compliment them on their physical beauty without flirting. Women need to be able to relate to men without feeling oppressed or taken advantage of, and without using their physical beauty to seduce men. God made us as sexual beings; we should rejoice in that and use his gift responsibly. The Bible gives an exciting and attractive image of healthy, committed relationships between men and women, taking full account of our physical beauty. This is the true image against which other false images like pornography must be assessed. We should be against pornography because we are for sex as God intended it.

2

Visual Prostitution

What is pornography?

The word pornography comes from the Greek and literally means 'the writing of [*or* about] whores'. It is generally accepted to cover a wide range of materials from magazines like *Playboy* and *Penthouse* to acts of great violence and cruelty involving women, children and in some cases men. The simplest definition which I have found useful is that coined in 1972 by the Longford Committee:

> that which exploits and dehumanises sex so that human beings are treated as things, and women, in particular, as sex objects.

In testing material against this definition I have found it helpful to ask three questions:

1. *How does it portray women?*

Pornographic material shows women to be a mere assemblage of physical parts with particular emphasis on the breasts and genitalia. There is little or no attempt to show the other aspects of a woman's character or strengths as a mental or spiritual being. As the feminist movement has so helpfully identified, much material often describes or displays women in subjective poses where men are in positions of power and dominance, and in the most extreme cases expressing that power through violence and rape.

2. How does the material show the sexual relationship?

Pornography invariably portrays sexual intercourse as the only aspect of a relationship between men and women. Pornography rarely, if ever, shows the sexual relationship in the loving, caring context of marriage. Love and commitment are words not found in pornographic material and children are never mentioned as resulting from sexual activity. Sex is available wherever you want it, whenever you want it and in whatever form you want it. Pornography is about consumption rather than giving. The idea that pornography can help the sexual relationship is a myth—short-term titillation is no substitute for long-term love and commitment.

3. What is the purpose of the material?

Material can have explicit sexual content without being pornographic. Examples are medical textbooks, and manuals designed to improve sexual technique (although there is an unfortunate trend in these towards perverted sexual activity). By contrast, pornography is not designed with an educational purpose. Its objective is to titillate, stimulate and provoke sexual desire.

What about Page 3?

I believe the answers to these three questions help us understand the difference between material that can have some constructive value, and that which is merely destructive. In these terms photographs like those on page 3 of *The Sun*, and in newspapers like *The Sport*, can rightly be defined as pornographic. Although such photographs do not show explicit sexual activity, nor usually the genital area, they do fail the test of treating women as more than mere physical beings. They put incredible emphasis on physical statistics (in particular the size of the breasts) rather than a woman's character as a whole. The brief accompanying text usually has some titillating overtone.

Clare Short, the Labour MP, describes how when she launched her parliamentary bill against photographs of topless women appearing in newspapers, she received a huge mailbag. Women from all backgrounds shared how they were affected by these photographs. Those with small breasts wrote how they felt humiliated; those with large breasts shared how they had become the butt of jokes and comments like 'You should be a Page 3 girl'; and most poignantly those with breast cancer who had had a mastectomy wrote of their hurt and offence. These letters have now been collected together in a book *Dear Clare*....[1]

What about art and erotica?

Applying my three-part test also helps in dealing with the issue of works of art and erotica. Consider the comments of a senior MP in a radio interview

about the difficulty of defining what was pornographic. He talked of how there was so much
nudity on the roof of the Cistine Chapel and
indeed in public buildings in Whitehall. Were
anti-pornographers against such works of art?

We must first recognise the importance of differences between various media. Photography is
realistic. A real living woman leaps out of the page.
Paintings or statues by comparison generally convey something deeper than 'surface realism'.
Moreover the physical beauty of a woman shown
naked in a statue or a painting does not convey the
same domination by men as is often shown in the
expressions on faces of women in magazines or on
video, nor does it have the same titillating and
provoking quality. Of course there are exceptions
which would fail the test because of their realism,
explicitness and intention. One example is the case
of a sculpture with a puppet-like caricature of Mrs
Thatcher for its face and an insect's body in a pose
of copulating with a map of Britain. This is unacceptable because of the linking of a real person in a
contorted sexual act.

The question is often posed, 'Are you against
erotica?' The difficulty in responding is to know
what the questioner means. The word is used very
loosely; some people might be thinking of a 'soft'
pornographic magazine, others of a sex manual.
Some would define erotica as material which
involves mutual caring sex between a man and a
woman. There is very little material of this nature
that would be of use for Christians. However,
there are some helpful sex manuals which talk
about the sexual relationship within the context of

marriage and do not gloss over important questions about sexual technique and sexual problems. Two examples I would recommend are *A Touch of Love* by John and Janet Houghton and *Intended for Pleasure* by Ed and Gaye Wheat.[2]

Whatever one's view of erotica, material which encourages sexual experimentation outside marriage cannot be condoned. For example, the popular *Joy of Sex* manual now includes a section on group sex. Much else of what is in the manual would be of help to Christians but this section is clearly not appropriate. Is it therefore pornography? I would say that in these specific sections it does have aspects of pornographic content. But that is a different question from whether it should be made illegal, something we will consider later in this chapter.

Is 'soft core' pornography acceptable?

People talk about 'hard core' and 'soft core' pornography as if they were two distinct, well defined categories of material. In fact the terms are used by different people in different ways. They are not legal terms. Most people think of hard pornography as anything which includes more explicit sexual action or violence, or sexual perversion, or children. Soft pornography is everything else. Language can be misleading. The adjective 'soft' gives the impression of acceptability. The pornographers want us to believe that the material is innocent, harmless, and by the word 'soft' even seek to associate it with the ideas of love and care and tenderness. Publishers and newsagents will make statements like, 'We are totally against hard-core pornography, but we will accept some softer material.' They usually do not want even to use the word 'pornography', preferring to talk about 'glamour magazines' or 'girlie magazines'.

An interesting example of the double thinking that goes on and the 'hardness' of some allegedly soft material is the case of the Henry Miller book *Opus Pistorum* also known as *Under the Roofs of Paris*. Henry Miller is a well-known author whose works are often studied as English literature. But *Opus Pistorum* contains a note explaining that Miller wrote the book at a time when he needed money and was paid by the page by a sex-shop owner. The book is a catalogue of extreme sexual activity. In 1988 CARE discovered it was being sold by W H Smith and other well-known booksellers. The police were unsure they would succeed in a legal action against the book because of the convention since the Williams Report in 1979 that the written word should not be acted against. I read the book in order to prepare a summary of it. I was horrified.

The book starts with a child of 13 having sex with a man and almost every page includes some sexual act. There is a detailed description of a gang rape and of bestiality. Paedophilia runs throughout the book. Buggery and oral sex are described in detail. In my view, to describe such material as 'soft' pornography is grossly misleading.

I sent my summary to the Chairman of W H Smith and then met with staff at their Head Office. Smiths were not willing to condemn the book outright, and argued that they could not be censors.

Intriguingly, however, they told me that they had decided to stop stocking the book 'for commercial reasons'.

The contents of pornography

A number of studies have been undertaken of the contents of pornography. Some of these have not been academic studies as such but more a record of the personal impressions of those who wanted to discover what was actually being sold and publicly available. One example is the article which appeared in *The Independent* in April 1989 by Catherine Itzin and Corinne Sweet, two feminists from the Campaign against Pornography and Censorship, who walked along a typical High Street in London purchasing all the pornographic magazines they could find in newsagents and other shops. They were shocked by what they found, particularly by representations of girls in so-called 'shaver magazines'.

> Child pornography is illegal in the UK, but we found adult women shaved to look like little girls. They were young, flat-chested, in white socks and sandals; they were posed to look child-like: photographed headless or from the waist down, or pouting, fingers in mouth. Wearing gingham dresses and straw hats, they were posed with legs tight together or vaginas exposed to the camera. What is being represented are female children inviting sexual access and what is being engineered is the sexual arousal of adult males by their bodies.

CARE undertook a similar exercise before

27

launching its campaign against pornography called 'Picking Up The Pieces' in 1988. We purchased about a dozen different examples of pornographic magazines within a few hundred yards of our offices in London. These magazines portrayed women as inviting and wanting sexual activity in many different situations—in the home, work place, hospital, street, at parties, from men that in most instances they hardly knew. The written text accompanying the photographs often described sexual activity with much greater explicitness. The combination of photographs and text is a very powerful and provocative stimulant. Both sex therapists and the police talk of their deep concern of the interaction between words and pictures. It was not an enjoyable exercise and not one we would recommend to others. Although we attempted to make it as clinical as possible, we were not immune from being titillated by the material. But at the end of the exercise our overwhelming feeling was one of numbness and sadness at this kind of portrayal of women.

The impact of the message that these magazines give about the nature of the sexual relationship is frightening. The situation is even worse when one looks at more explicit material. This is starkly conveyed by Park Dietz, a psychiatrist who served as Commissioner on the 1986 US Attorney General's Commission on Pornography (known as the Meese Commission). He undertook a survey of pornography for the Commission and summarised his findings as follows:

A person who learned about human sexuality in the

'adults only' pornography outlets of America would be a person who had never conceived of a man and woman marrying or even falling in love before having intercourse, who had never conceived of two people making love in privacy without guilt or fear of discovery, who had never conceived tender foreplay, who had never conceived of vaginal intercourse with ejaculation during intromission, and who had never conceived of procreation as a purpose of sexual union. Instead, such a person would be one who had learned that sex at home meant sex with one's children, step-children, parents, step-parents, siblings, cousins, nephews, nieces, aunts, uncles and pets and with neighbours, milkmen, plumbers, salesmen, burglars and peepers, who had learned that people take off their clothes to have sex within the first five minutes of meeting one another, who had learned to misjudge the percentage of women who prepare for sex by shaving their pubic hair, having their breasts, buttocks or legs tattooed, having their nipples or labia pierced, or donning leather, latex, rubber or childlike costumes.[3]

The Attorney General's Commission rejected the terms 'hard' and 'soft' material as an inadequate means of describing content. Instead they used five different categories to examine sexually explicit material: sexually violent; non-violent but degrading; non-violent and non-degrading; nudity; child pornography. Of these five categories, only in the case of nudity could the Commission unanimously conclude that the material was not harmful. Differing opinions were held about non-violent and non-degrading materials. Violent, degrading, and child pornography were all unanimously opposed.

When we ordinarily talk of violence we may think of beating or smacking. Pornographic magazines of the more extreme kind can include the most sadistic violence involving the insertion of sharp objects into a woman's body, the actual physical maiming of parts of the body, torture and violent rape. In a 1990 court case following an operation by the police, code named 'Operation Spanner', a group of men were sentenced for engaging in violent and sadomasochistic activities on each other and recording these in photographs and video tape. The police originally started their operation because they found pornographic material showing activities they thought individuals could not survive. For example, male sexual organs were attacked with hammers and nails and wire brushes. When the Head of Scotland Yard's Obscene Publication Squad described these activities to a group of MPs at a seminar organised by CARE, there was an audible wincing in the audience.

Legal verses illegal

When talking about pornography we need to separate out the questions of what makes something pornographic, what is the content of pornographic material, and what makes it illegal. They are different issues. Some people think that we should only be concerned about material if it is illegal. Others feel that when we are trying to define pornography we are trying to define what the police should be concerned about. There is, however, much material which is not technically illegal but about which we should still be concerned. As Christians we should be quick to grasp this concept. Although the law in the Old Testament was able to present a code of conduct of what was right and wrong, Jesus explained that the law was not adequate in determining what our response should be to situations and how our attitudes should be moulded. The law can only go so far.

In addition, there are a number of other important constraints on the law:

(a) It must be clear. The law cannot cope with grey areas or areas of debate. It has to define clear standards against which material can be measured.

(b) The law has to be enforceable. There is no point in having a definition that appears clear if it is not workable in practice.

(c) The law has to fit into the legal traditions of a particular country.

For this reason legal definitions of what is pornographic will vary from country to country. This is a specialised area of debate and not one that should inhibit practical action against pornography at a local level. The newsagent may be right when he says that the material he stocks is legal. But that should not stop us from convincing him that he is stocking material which is not healthy and may cause harm. *What we should strive for in the legal area is the clearest possible definition that captures the widest possible range of pornographic material with the minimum possible loss of freedom to publish.*

This may become clearer if we consider an analogy. Imagine that a gun club has set up a firing range on some open countryside close to a village. Local people are very concerned about the danger involved, although the gun club defend their activities as a private matter. Attempts to declare the gun club activities completely illegal fail, but a campaign to put up a fence around the firing ranges follows. The fence would prevent onlookers, and in particular children, from straying into the danger area. Agreement is reached that a fence should be built, but there is disagreement about *where* the fence should be. The club wants to put a short fence immediately around the core of the activities. Local people want a much wider area covered to prevent stray bullets going over the fence. In the end a compromise deal is struck but bullets still sometimes stray over the fence. Local people therefore maintain a publicity campaign to make people aware of the dangers of going anywhere near the area.

No analogy is perfect. The parallel between the activities of a properly constituted gun club and the production of pornography is not precise. But the point is that the debate about legal and illegal pornography is similar to the question of where the fence should be built. In our analogy even after the fence is put up there is still potential for harm from stray bullets. In the case of pornography harm can come from so-called 'softer' material which lies outside the 'fence', either purchased knowingly or found by others. We will need to maintain a campaign even when a legal definition has been settled: 'the fence' cannot do the whole job.

The analogy also helps in dealing with the question of those like the W H Smith executives I mentioned earlier, who argue that we should not have censorship. The word 'censorship' has become something of a sacred cow for libertarians. In fact it is something that we all do every day of our lives. We are constantly faced with decisions of where to draw the line. Are those against censorship really arguing there should be no line at all? Are they arguing that child pornography and violent material should be allowed? Very, very few people would do so in public in Britain today. No, the true subject of debate is where the line should be drawn. We are all in favour of censorship to some extent. It is merely a question of what should be censored and by what process that decision is reached.

3

A Bit of Harmless Fun?

The question of whether, and how, pornography is harmful has been a vexed area of debate for more than twenty years. It has been the subject of a stream of official reports both in the UK and the USA. It has led to sharp and at times emotive disagreement between people. I have weighed this issue carefully and am convinced that pornography does have serious negative effects to which society must respond. You will have to make up your own mind. This chapter examines directly the public evidence for the harm pornography causes. The following chapter assesses the material itself from the Christian perspective.

The difficulty with the 'harms' debate is that we are often swayed by banner headlines like 'Study says no link between pornography and sex crime'. We need to understand that it is very difficult to prove conclusively cause and effect in any social science research. Research projects investigating the impact of pornography are subject to additional limitations. It is impossible to recreate in the carefully controlled environment of the laboratory the circumstances leading to sexual crime. Indeed it would be unethical for a researcher to attempt to undertake such an exercise. Questions about the impact of pornography should not be posed in terms of absolute proof, but rather in terms of what conclusions are justified by the weight of evidence. Furthermore, it is essential that such evidence be wide-ranging. It needs to include the testimony of people who have been addicted to pornography, and of those who have suffered as victims because of other people's addiction. We need to listen to those who work with sexual offenders: the police, prison officers, and therapists. We should look at academic studies of offenders as well as studies that have taken place in the laboratory. Finally we need to consider evidence from studies of how sex crime rates have varied. It is the combined weight of this evidence that will help us understand the problem. To concentrate on narrow academic evidence alone is like confining medical research on a new virus to laboratory work rather than looking at the patients and personal histories of those affected.

Testimony of users

CARE has received a number of letters from men who use pornography. The main feature that they point to is that it is addictive. Users find the habit very hard to break. One man wrote, 'I seem to always need one [a pornographic magazine] and the more I bought the more I wanted and the more I wanted the more I bought.' Another letter described how a man started purchasing magazines at the age of 16, gradually bought 'harder' magazines and eventually would spend over £40 on a single visit to a sex shop. These men were not directly involved in any illegal activity or criminal offence, although they, and others who have written and talked to me, mention the deadening effect of pornography on their lives in relationships with women. Another man described how purchasing the material gradually changed the way he viewed women. This man, who was not a Christian, had a regular sexual partner. The pornography that he saw, however, made him dissatisfied with his sexual relationship and with his partner. He craved for more excitement and a more physically attractive partner. Another man explained to me how he became so engrossed in pornography that he could not contemplate a normal sexual relationship—he consumed sex through pornography and visiting prostitutes.

At a more graphic level the personal testimony of sex offenders helps us understand the impact pornography can have. The most noteworthy example is that of Ted Bundy. Bundy was executed on the 24 January 1989 at Florida State Prison for a series of murders associated with sexual assault and rape. The night before he was executed he gave an interview to Dr James Dobson, the child psychiatrist who heads up the Focus on the Family ministry in the USA. Bundy had heard of Dr Dobson because he had read the full report of the Attorney General's Commission on Pornography in the USA on which Dr Dobson was a Commissioner. After some correspondence he felt he had built up a relationship with Dobson to the degree that he could trust him to record an interview immediately prior to his death. The result was the most remarkable visual record of a man facing death and wanting to talk about the influence pornography had had on his life. Anyone concerned about pornography should obtain a copy of this video (available from CARE).

Bundy explains how he first came across pornography as a young boy of 12 or 13 in local shops. From this 'softer' material he later moved on to 'harder' material found in the neighbourhood amongst people's rubbish and in other places. When he was old enough he frequented specialist sex stores and bought more extreme pornography. He gradually became addicted to increasingly more explicit material. Bundy had been brought up in a good home, was married and held down a responsible job as a legal assistant. He was an apparently stable and normal individual. In the interview he did not blame pornography in the sense that he might want to relinquish responsibility for his crimes. On the contrary he fully recognised the horror of what he had done, but wanted to warn others about the damage that pornography can do and the role that it can play in sexual offences. He described how eventually the 'hardest' pornography lost the thrill for him that it had initially had, and that he felt that only acting out the incidents he had seen would bring the pleasure he sought. After a battle for some two years with his conscience and inner desires he eventually gave in and committed a serious sexual assault.

In one telling part of the interview Bundy talks

about his experience in prison and compares that with what some social scientists say about pornography. He says, 'Listen, I'm no social scientist and I haven't done a survey...but I have lived in prison for a long time now. And I've met a lot of men who were motivated to commit violence just like me. And without exception every one of them was deeply involved in pornography—without question, without exception—deeply influenced and consumed by an addiction to pornography.'

Personal testimony of victims

Those who suffer as a result of pornography are sometimes in a position to talk about what happened. An important collection of material of this type is found in the book published by 'Everywoman' in 1988, 'Pornography and Sexual Violence', which is a transcript of public hearings held in Minneapolis in 1985. Some witnesses quoted direct evidence of sexual offences, for example a woman who was raped as an adolescent by three men and later saw that they had been reading pornographic magazines in their camp nearby. Other witnesses whose partners were addicted to pornography described the degrading influence on the patterns of their sexual behaviour. One woman eventually sought help after she had been left hanging upside down in her bedroom even though her young child was in the house and crying. There has been no systematic attempt in the UK to collect evidence of victims and CARE believes it would be a significant breakthrough if such an exercise were undertaken in a confidential and reliable manner. Individual testimony does need careful assessment, but nonetheless the overall import of such evidence is likely to demonstrate the terrorising impact that pornography can have.

Testimony of those who work with offenders

We also need to take account of those who work closely with people who have committed sexual offences. In the UK one name constantly crops up in relation to this kind of work—Ray Wyre. Ray was a probation officer who gradually specialised in working with sex offenders, especially in Albany Prison on the Isle of Wight. Eventually he was so concerned about the lack of help such people received that he decided with others to set up a private clinic, Gracewell Clinic in Birmingham, to provide a programme of therapy. Ray is deeply concerned about pornography and his concern is rooted in practical experience. He spoke at a seminar which CARE organised for MPs and peers in the Houses of Parliament in January 1989.[4] Ray points to the 'normalising' impact that the sale of pornography has on offenders—that is, offenders believe that *all* women are available for sexual activity because that is what they see from the pages of pornographic magazines. He compellingly argues that some men will never commit sexual offences as a result of looking at pornography; and some men will commit sexual offences whether they have seen pornography or not; but there is a large group in the middle who may be influenced by pornography and become much more likely to commit offences.

Studies of sex offenders

A bridge between this kind of practical testimony and the more academic research is provided by those who have had long-term experience of working with sex offenders and then sought to use their experiences as a basis for research. One such worker is Dr Victor Cline, a psychiatrist at the University of Utah in the USA. Having dealt with over 300 sex offenders Cline developed his model of what he believed to be the impact of pornography in their pattern of offending.[5] He concluded that there were four steps:

(1) *Addiction*—typically offenders became addicted to pornography, some at an early age.

(2) *Escalation*—as with other addictions there was a gradual escalation in the kind of material which offenders purchased. They moved from 'soft' to 'hard' pornography.

(3) *Desensitisation*—as more and more material was consumed offenders became less affected by the material they saw. They found it more difficult to distinguish between what would be considered acceptable behaviour and what would be considered unacceptable. The distinctions between right and wrong became blurred. They became less and less excited by watching pornography.

(4) *Acting out*—the final stage was when offenders no longer contained what they saw in pornography as an experience of mental excitement but went out and sought real women to use in living out their sexual fantasies.

Cline's work is built on hard experience, not on the isolated evidence of a Ted Bundy. These conclusions are supported by Marshall's work with sex offenders in Canada.[6]

Studies of the incidence of sexual crime

There has been much controversy about the proposition that if pornography is less available in a society the level of sexual crime will drop. A leading worker in this field has been Dr John Court who, in the late 70s and early 80s, undertook a number of studies.[7] Perhaps Court's most effective contribution was to discredit the earlier work of Ben Kutchinski who had sought to prove that the liberalisation of the anti-pornography laws in Denmark had led to a drop in sexual crime. It is now generally accepted that Kutchinski's work was grossly misleading not least because the definition of sexual crime had changed over the same period in which there had been a drop.

But Court also undertook studies comparing the rape rates and sale of pornography in different countries. Some of the comparisons are striking, but this area of research suffers from a number of drawbacks. Not only is it very difficult to ensure that sexual crime statistics are counted and interpreted in the same way in different countries (or even areas of the same country) but also it is a complex matter at this global level to establish what may have influenced a falling or rising crime rate other than the level of pornography. We should be wary of drawing rigorous conclusions solely on the basis of studies which correlate different statistics. What can be compelling, however, is small-scale studies of particular well-defined areas where the statistics are collected by the same police force immediately before and after a change. One example is in Oklahoma in the USA, where following a crackdown on the sale of pornography in Oklahoma City the rape rate fell, whereas in Oklahoma County where no such crackdown had taken place the level remained the same and indeed rose.[8]

Academic laboratory study

There has been much controversy about *academic* studies of the impact of pornography. Often such studies have involved showing pornographic material to students in university psychology laboratories and assessing their reactions in a number of different ways. This kind of study formed an important part of the review of research undertaken by Dr Dennis Howitt and Dr Guy Cumberbatch at the request of the Home Office in 1990. The review was a direct result of an Early Day Motion signed by 243 MPs expressing concern about the continuing sale of pornography, and calling for a study on its impact. CARE was closely involved in helping MPs with this motion which was sponsored by six MPs of all parties.

Howitt and Cumberbatch concluded that 'evidence of the adverse effects of pornography is far less clear-cut than some earlier reviews imply. Inconsistencies emerge between very similar studies and many interpretations of these have reached almost opposite conclusions.' The Cumberbatch and Howitt view is hotly contested by academics. Of course, there have been disagreements about

43

what effect pornography has when viewed as part of a laboratory experiment. It is reasonable to conclude however that, taken as a whole, such research does point to a negative effect.

Certain academic studies have been especially important in pointing to the negative effect of pornography. One example is the work of Dr Dolf Zillman of the University of Alabama.[9] Zillman has carried out a number of studies on the effect of adult non-violent and violent pornography. One of his experiments involved showing a series of pornographic films over a six-week period to volunteer students. These students were independently surveyed for their attitudes towards women prior to and after the study, and the conclusions show that they developed an increased callousness towards women, a tendency to trivialise rape as a criminal offence, a tendency to develop distorted perceptions about sexuality and an appetite for more deviant bizarre or violent types of pornography. I have visited Zillman and he told me that he was convinced that the negative effects of pornography had been more consistently proven than the links between smoking and lung cancer. It seems incredible that Zillman's most recent review of research, including works from a number of authors published in 1989, was not taken into account by the Home Office study.

Another very significant study is that undertaken by James Weaver at the University of Auburn, also in Alabama. Weaver went to enormous lengths to eliminate any possible bias from his study which was designed to establish what impact very limited exposure of soft pornography would have on students' attitudes towards women. His concern was to avoid the accusation that is sometimes levelled at such research that psychology students will understand the purpose of experiments and give the results, even subconsciously, that they think the researcher wants. Weaver personally avoided any direct contact with the students during any of the exercises. Control groups were carefully constructed and exercises structured so that the connection between the viewing of pornography and the subsequent questions was hidden. Weaver's research demonstrated that those who had seen pornography were much more likely to view women as sex objects, and when presented with a typical rape scenario would recommend a much lighter sentence than those who had not seen pornography.[10]

It is right to adopt a cautious approach in interpreting academic research on this subject. A small number of studies do not prove or demonstrate strong links between pornography and negative effects. The effects of different kinds of material will vary. Not everyone who is exposed to pornography will react in the same way. But, even given the limitations of such research, the overall assessment must be that pornography has shown a negative effect.

Summary of effects

Taking all these different kinds of evidence together, the harmful effects of pornography can be summarised:

1. *General attitudes to women*

The availability of pornography in our society and its consumption by men contribute to a lowering of the general attitude towards women and a belief that they are sexually available. This was illustrated for me when I was returning from Manchester on a Saturday evening with a colleague from a CARE conference. As we sat in the train at Manchester station three young football fans came into the compartment each carrying a pornographic magazine. As they sat down in the seats behind us we could hear them talking about the contents of the magazines. Then a very attractive young woman joined the train and sat level with my companion and me. One of the fans looked up from his magazine and said to the others in a sniggering tone, 'Cor, look, a woman.' It is hard to convey in the printed word the degree of sexual undertone he managed to invest in that short phrase. I know that if I had been that woman I would have felt very intimidated by those young men.

2. *Attitudes to the sexual relationship*

Pornography promotes a false image of the sexual relationship without love and commitment. It promotes the idea of constant and complete sexual satisfaction. Such satisfaction at the level that pornography describes it is a myth. Of course (as described in Chapter 1) the sexual relationship is a wonderfully satisfying aspect of the whole relationship between a man and a woman. But the sexual relationship is not and never can be the diet of easy continual ecstasy that pornography would have us believe in. Pornography promotes destructive fantasy and can damage the ability of men to have a proper sexual relationship and ruin the mutual love and respect which should characterise sex within marriage.

3. Impact on sex offenders

Evidence from offenders like Ted Bundy and professionals like Ray Wyre and Victor Cline clearly demonstrate that pornography *does* contribute to the development of a pattern of sexual crime.

4. Direct use in offences

A final kind of harm is where pornography is used directly by offenders to 'soften up' victims, or describes sexual activity which is copied by offenders in their crimes. The saddest cases are those involving children. For example, Leicester Crown Court was told in January 1989 of the offence of a 31-year-old man who indecently assaulted his girlfriend's 8-year-old daughter after showing her a pornographic magazine. In such cases pornography is used to justify the abuse, and children are persuaded that if adults take off their clothes and do certain things to each other then it is legitimate. Another example is of the Putney Rapist jailed for 18 years in 1988 for a series of sex attacks. The court was told that he was obsessed with bondage and the degradation of women. The police said he copied ideas for rape from illustrations in a bondage magazine called *The Trap*.

Pornography is not the only evil in our society, nor do we fully understand how individuals are affected by it. But the weight of evidence is sufficient for us to conclude that pornography causes considerable harm and plays an important role in some sex offences. It is right to be cautious in interpreting academic evidence, but nonetheless this type of research does show the negative effects of pornography. Even the weak and controversial Home Office report on pornography concludes:

> There is a good deal of justification for the association of pornography with social ills in the public mind: pornography is part of the sexual abuse of children, battered wives seem more likely to be pressurized by pornography, some sexual offenders use pornography as part of the preparation for their crimes, the breakdown of the family is more common where pornography is prevalent, the traditional family is vulnerable in many of these societies where pornography is pervasive, and so forth.[11]

4

The Need to Respond

For some the only issue that matters in relation to pornography is whether it directly causes measurable harm. This was the position that the Williams Committee took in 1979, putting enormous emphasis on so-called scientific evidence such as that we examined in the last chapter. For the Christian the argument goes beyond the damaging effects of pornography already identified. Pornography does affect sexual offenders; it is associated with sexual crime; it is used to 'soften up' children in preparation for abuse; it is used in some relationships as a pre-cursor to violent attack. But these are merely branches of the tree of pornographic evil.

The root lies in the false image which pornography peddles both of the nature of women and of the sexual relationship. One of the most important gains in recent years among Christians is a rediscovery of the importance and value which God ascribes to women. Women have individual dignity as whole human beings. Women have a specific and complementary role to that of men both in marriage and in the wider community. But in no way can women be described as being of lesser value, worth, esteem or honour compared with the male of the species. Indeed, the Bible leads us to suggest the opposite. Against this ideal, pornography brings out a message of lies and false images. Women's only value in pornography is their physical attractiveness. It is the size of their breasts, the shape of their bodies, the availability of their genitalia that matter in pornography. Pornographic material never gives you an insight or impression of an individual's character. It is as if personality is irrelevant. Intelligence is of no consequence. A very narrow interpretation of beauty is provided. Pornography is women's bodies for sale.

Furthermore, pornography displays women as playthings. Men are seen as the dominant party. Women are portrayed as those whose purpose is to gratify male sexual desire. It is as if women have no preference or choice or active decision-making role. Material does exist with images of women seducing men, but what is presented is mindless female bodies with avaricious appetites for sexual intercourse.

The dominance theme in extreme cases is mixed with violence. Explicit sexual violence in pornography is illegal in the UK. There are, however, magazines and videos available that contain strong hints of violence. Implements are left lying around in pictures and sharp objects are pressed close to genital areas although not inserted. Women are decked with chains and whips. Much

THE NEED TO RESPOND

is left to the imagination but the overriding message conveys an invitation for men to dominate women. No such imagination is required in the more extreme material that can be purchased under the counter or through illegal mail-order networks. In such material men are depicted showing extreme cruelty and violence towards women. Ted Bundy (see pages 37-39) talks of the impact of slasher movies—films involving extreme violence against women where they are subjugated by torture. Such material is utterly degrading towards women. But we need to be aware that the theme of dominance runs through pornography right from the most extremely violent material to the subtle implications found in Page 3 photographs. Men are bigger and better and wiser than women and the only thing women are good for is sexual acts.

We have outlined how pornography promotes a false image of women. We must also consider how pornography destroys the image the Bible promotes of the sexual relationship. In pornography sex is portrayed as a commodity. It is a consumer product like any other. Pornographic magazines are like commercial catalogues, except instead of *What Car?* or *What Holiday?* we have *What Woman?*. As we have seen in Chapter 1, God's intention is different. The sexual relationship was part of the ultimate purpose of God's creation. It was and is the fusion of man and woman in the context of love and commitment and faithfulness. Pornography is the opposite of this.

As part of my work I have appeared in a number of radio and television programmes about pornography. On one occasion I was involved in a two-hour discussion on a local radio station which was accompanied by a telephone vote as to whether the listeners thought pornography was harmful. On the programme was a female editor of a leading pornography and 'contact' magazine. The magazine's format is of a number of explicit sexual articles accompanied by small photographs of individuals, usually partly clothed, both men and women who are looking for sexual contact with others.

The discussion in the programme was lively. I was sitting beside the magazine editor, and half-way through the programme we had a ten-minute break in the recording. As we talked I recall silently praying for an opportunity to pierce her veneer of professional commitment to her job and dismissiveness towards those who opposed pornography. She told me that she was shortly to get married to her boyfriend. Reacting to an inner impulse I asked her whether she expected that her husband would be faithful to her. She was indignant, 'But of course!' she replied. I then pointed out that her magazine did nothing to encourage faithfulness, rather the opposite in its portrayal of sex as a commodity. She tried to offer some defence, but it was sadly obvious that the comment had hit home.

Pornography rips the sexual relationship from its proper context and reduces it to a mere question of technique. Instead of a healthy discussion with their wives about matters like frequency of intercourse and sexual technique, men are prompted by pornography to seek constant sexual satisfaction often by degrading means. This damages both marriage partners. It creates a gnawing emptiness within men as they strive for an elusive and false image of sexual perfection.

This is graphically illustrated by the experience of Ron and Maureen Sims. Ron is a lovely man from a rough, tough background who got involved in the pornography industry in the early days. He made a considerable amount of money through selling pornographic magazines. But it began to impact his relationship with his wife, and he dragged her into a life of virtual prostitution. He enjoyed watching her have sex with other men. Then Ron became a Christian, and later so did his wife. There was a transformation in their lives, a healing, a forgiveness and a new sexual purity. They learned to love each other again when love had gone out of their relationship.[12]

But men do not need to go to those extremes to be affected by pornography. Another area of negative impact which is almost impossible to measure but nonetheless potent is that of sexual fantasy. Pornography feeds into that area of our minds and spirits that dreams dreams and constructs fantasy. The Bible recognises the enormous potential within the human mind to be provoked by literally fantastic imagery to a sense of awe and wonder. If challenging imagery were removed from Scripture we would lose a substantial part of the Bible, including the prophecies of Isaiah and Jeremiah, and the imagery of Daniel, Ezekiel and Revelation. Scripture also contains many word pictures of the coming King Jesus as the Lamb, the Lion, the Shepherd, the King. In our own day C. S. Lewis has demonstrated in his *Chronicles of Narnia* how powerful fantasy can be. But the problem with pornography is that it feeds sexual fantasy with negative images. It unlocks a negative fantasy realm in our minds that gets us on to an unhealthy track and isolates our thinking. It blocks out the real world through seeking to feed selfish sexual arousal alone.

For the Christian the antidote to all of this is to return to the Bible and look at God's intention and to enjoy all that he created for us in a positive way. If we are single we can learn to appreciate the opposite sex without recourse to sexual fantasy. Women can be appreciated as whole women and men as whole men. This does not ignore physical beauty but puts it into the right context. If we are married we can rediscover, as Ron and Maureen Sims did, the joy of a whole relationship replacing the void created by pornography.

But all of this begs the important question as to what kind of public response Christians should make to pornography. A later chapter looks at practical initiatives which can be taken, but it is appropriate here briefly to refer to the principles on which any action should be based:

1. Direct your anger properly

It is right to be angered by pornography because of the destruction that it brings. Anger is an appropriate Christian emotion. It may be helpful to imagine the fury Jesus felt in the Temple (because it was being misused as a market place) being similarly aroused in us today. Indeed the parallels are close. The Bible talks much about the temples of our human bodies and Paul uses that imagery in relation to sexual purity in 1 Corinthians 6:18–20. We are too accepting and complacent about the changes that pornography brings. We do need to rise up in anger. But like Jesus we must channel our anger in the right way. It is pornography itself that needs to be challenged and the people who produce it. The major producers of pornography know what they are doing. A small newsagent may be selling pornography without being aware of its content. We must be careful not to lambast many who sell it as a small part of their business without realising the repercussions. I have known examples of newsagents tearing up magazines on the spot when they discovered what was in them.

2. Love the victims

Pornography has many victims—the woman trapped in a relationship who is forced to imitate pornography by her partner; the child who has been seduced by pornography and then abused; and the victims of sexual attack where pornography was involved. Such people need love, care and acceptance in addition to professional help. Individual Christians and churches can provide the support necessary to help rebuild broken lives.

In another sense those addicted to pornography are victims, although they are obviously responsible for their actions. The final chapter of this book is addressed particularly to such 'addicts'. The success of an individual fighting this habit, however, often depends to a considerable degree on the willingness of Christians to accept and support them as they labour under a huge burden of guilt.

3. Don't campaign on your own

This book may already have prompted you to want to do something to fight the evil of pornography. But it is vital that such action is carefully planned. Apart from one or two instances where an immediate reaction may be necessary, it is much better that action be taken by two or more people. Pornography is a powerful force and unfortunately it is all too easy for those who try to do something against it to become entrapped themselves. There is strength in numbers, and the encouragement to take a more clinical approach. (See Chapter 8 below.)

4. Don't campaign only on pornography

For similar reasons I encourage individuals and groups not to focus solely on pornography. It is important to have other interests to balance a campaign on this issue. This is not an argument against groups that have been set up specifically to combat pornography, but more a plea to ensure that there is a varied life outside of fighting this issue.

5. Pray

Any action by Christians must be underpinned by prayer. The power of pornography is not limited to the page or film on which it is recorded visually. Spiritual protection is vital in combating the issue. Equally it is vital to pray for those who are trapped and affected by the industry.

As Christians we must see beyond the written page to the underlying forces of pornography. We must counter the false imagery conveyed in pornography and combat it with positive images.

5

Where There's Muck There's Brass

At least one industry in the UK seems to have survived the ups and downs of the economy over the last thirty years and gone from strength to strength. Pornography sales are big business involving many millions of pounds each year. Unlike other commercial sectors, however, it is almost impossible to obtain the normal business data to chart the growth and change in the industry. Pornographers seem happy to bank their takings without worrying about proving how well they have done. At least in part this is because they fund many of their developments without recourse to the financial institutions that require the kind of published data we have come to expect from other industries. There are no analysts on the Stock Market specialising in the pornography sector, even though its sales in the UK are in excess of a hundred million pounds per annum. It is a shady business which often runs close to the law or other attempts to regulate it.

To understand the industry better we need to

examine the main types of pornography, the main distribution outlets and the trends in the business.

Types of pornography

There are nine main media which include pornography in some form in Britain today:

Newspapers

Twenty years ago although the popular press in Britain did serve up a diet of stories with the main purpose of titillation, there was no visual nudity. All that changed with the circulation wars of the 1970s when *The Sun* newspaper, followed by *The Star*, introduced the concept of Page 3 and topless models. These newspapers have huge circulations, with *The Sun* exceeding four million copies. It is the most widely read paper in Britain today. Page 3 has become an institution which is widely accepted by the public. We owe a deep debt of gratitude to Clare Short MP for highlighting how women (and many men too) feel about Page 3. It is tragic that when she first introduced her Bill into the House of Commons to ban indecent displays in newspapers she was vilified by some male MPs as a spoilsport; *The Sun* itself started a campaign against 'crazy Clare'.

The Sun is not the worst example. The establishment of *The Sport* newspaper in 1986 by David Sullivan, a leading pornographer, has introduced even lower standards in a newspaper format. *The Sport* initially appeared on Sundays but is now available on weekdays as well. Part of its circulation is a cult following because of its lunatic stories like 'World War II bomber found on the moon', or 'Vision of Virgin Mary seen on Princess Diana's finger nails'.

But overall the contents stand somewhere between *The Sun* and a pornographic magazine. The letters page includes specific instances of sexual activities; the advertisements are mainly for pornographic magazines, sex shops, videos and telephone messages; and instead of a Page 3 picture, we have more explicit pictures of scantily dressed girls on nearly every other page. The majority of the stories have a sexual angle. There is a strong temptation to take an action against the paper under the Trade Description Act for calling itself a *news*paper, and sometimes even a 'family newspaper'! In March 1990 the Press Council, following numerous complaints, recommended that *The Sport* should not be treated as a newspaper but should be confined to the top shelf, alongside pornographic magazines. While it is helpful that the newspaper industry should reach such a conclusion, they appear little more than well-meaning words. The Press Council (now replaced by the Press Complaints Commission) has no teeth to enforce its ruling and most newsagents seem hardly even aware that it has happened. In any case, it is not easy to put a newspaper on a top shelf: unless it is folded and wrapped it inevitably slides and therefore it remains firmly on the bottom shelf where it is easily purchased by anyone, including children. On more than one occasion red-faced sports fanatics have bought the paper and brought it home only to discover to their horror that it had nothing to do with sport (in fact the sports coverage is feeble compared with other papers) and everything to do with pornography.

Books

In 1979 the Williams Committee concluded that 'the printed word should be neither restricted nor prohibited since its nature makes it neither immediately offensive nor capable of involving the harms we identify, because of its importance in conveying ideas.'[13] They were grossly mistaken in reaching this conclusion. The case of the Henry Miller book *Opus Pistorum* which was openly sold on the shelves of W H Smith is described on page 26. When I visited senior staff of W H Smith to discuss this book they admitted that they did sell a class of book which they recognised was merely intended to titillate. They did not consider it pornographic as such, preferring to talk of erotic literature. The books clearly sell sufficiently well to justify their place on W H Smith's shelves. But they do not have a storyline; instead there is an unremitting diet of different kinds of sexual activity. Such material is almost as dangerous as visual imagery because it encourages negative sexual fantasy. These books present a false image of women's sexual availability, are degrading and encourage men to live out their fantasies.

Another difficulty faced by those who go to purchase a paperback thriller novel is finding a book without a steamy sex scene. While such books are not pornography in the accepted sense, they do provide evidence of the general slide in standards towards a constant interest in the sexual. Another book, *The Sex Maniac's Diary*, is in a different league. This provides descriptions of different positions for sexual intercourse on each week of the year and a digest of information. Most worrying it includes the names and addresses and contact numbers for paedophilia organisations and other groups condoning different forms of sexual perversion. If you ever see this publication in a shop you should ask the manager to remove it from sale.

Magazines

Magazines are the most significant medium used by pornographers today. While the moving image, eg videos, may have a more lasting effect, magazines are the single most readily available kind of pornography which serve every available taste and perversion. They represent the gateway to the pornography industry. They are easily purchased and easily disposed of. They require no special equipment to be viewed and shared with others. They carry advertisements for 'harder' material, contact networks, mail order and sex shops. A small number of titles carry very high sales, eg *Men Only*, *Playboy*, *Fiesta*, *Club*, *Escort* and *Mayfair*. These high circulation titles are carried by the big chains (although W H Smith carry a more limited range), but the average smaller newsagent will stock a dozen or more titles. CARE local groups have found newsagents selling at least 50 different titles, taking up not only the top shelf but the second shelf as well and catering for every conceivable taste.

Comics

In recent years there has been a trend towards sexually explicit comics. Some of these reflect schoolboy toilet humour, eg *Viz*, but others have a more explicit pornographic content. The comics are aimed at adults not children, although there is nothing to stop a child buying them. A number of parents have contacted CARE to express their disgust on purchasing a magazine for their child, maybe at an airport or railway station, only to discover the contents. The worst examples often mix a religious theme with explicit sexuality. Material purchased in Oxford Street in London includes rape, drawings of sexual activities which would be illegal were they photographs, and violence with huge amounts of blood being shown. It is also disturbing that some of the main pornographic magazines, eg *Fiesta*, are now being produced in a comic format. This is a category which needs to be monitored closely.

Films

Explicit sexual material was first seen in the modern media in the 1960s and 70s on film. Special sex cinemas sprang up to show such films, some of which were very poorly made on 8mm film. Gradually films have been subject to increasing regulation, and now the sex cinema has almost died out with the advent of video. Although a large number of films with an '18' category do include gratuitous sex scenes, in the main films do not pose the problem they once did. This is simply because video tapes have superseded films as a means of cheap, easy distribution of pornographic material.

Videos

This has been a major growth area for pornography in the last ten years, owing to the explosion in sales of video recording equipment and the relative cheapness of tapes. Some 50% of homes in the UK now have video recorders. Following great concern in the early 1980s about video nasties with violent and explicit sexual content, a fairly effective system of regulation was set up by the 1984 Video Recordings Act. This provided for a statutory body (the role was given to the British Board of Film Classification) to classify every single video that would be sold or hired in the UK. A special category of 'restricted' video was introduced, the 'R18', which included explicit sexual content. Such videos could only be purchased or hired in licensed sex shops (of which more later). This 'R18' category tended to protect the ordinary adult '18' category from much pornographic content.

However, CARE has become very concerned about the attitude of BBFC to the 'R18' category. The BBFC have argued that because there are fewer sex shops (as a result of concerted campaigning from CARE and others at a local level), they are under pressure to recategorise videos they might consider 'R18' as '18', to thus enable them to be sold in a normal video hire shop. We believe the BBFC have got it wrong and that if sex shops should wither on the vine as a result of local pressure then the 'R18' category of video should be allowed to wither too.

The Video Retailers Association has done a tremendous job in cleaning up the act of many video shops, so that the industry which was born with the stigma associated with video nasties and piracy has now been adopted more into the main stream with a very helpful emphasis on the needs of families. In some areas Christians have taken a lead in this, for example the pioneering work of the Family Viewing outlet in Belfast.

However, the seamier side of life remains, not in mainstream video retailers but in small outlets and some sex shops where material may be sold with the wrong classification or no classification at all— both are offences under the Video Recordings Act. Video is also an important medium for 'hard core' pornography involving violence and children, with home-made material circulating widely. Often 'hard-core' tapes may be imported and then copied in quite large numbers which are sold through small advertisements in pornographic magazines.

Television

The main channels on British television (BBC1, BBC2, Independent Television and Channel 4) do not show the type of pornography that can be purchased on video or seen in a pornographic magazine. However, television programmes can present problems when they portray sex in a negative manner, or constantly refer to sexual innuendo, or depict incidents of unnecessarily explicit sexual content. It is largely due to the work of Mary Whitehouse OBE and the National Viewers' and Listeners' Association that the situation is not much worse. Mary is an outstanding example of a campaigner who started as a concerned citizen, recognised the sliding standards, and has fought tenaciously over twenty-five years to prevent things from getting worse. The establishment of the Broadcasting Standards Council with a specific remit to monitor sex and violence on television and radio and deal with complaints is, in some ways, the culmination of Mary's work.

The greatest threat to standards on television probably now lies with new channels that will come into operation over the next few years. These will include small cable channels, some of which are already operating, satellite services based in the UK like British Sky Broadcasting, and perhaps most worrying of all, satellite services based in Europe but transmitting to the UK. The regulation regime is tighter in the UK than in other countries, particularly the USA, where 'hard-core' pornography has been shown on some cable channels. It is more likely here that the problem will initially arise from European satellites beaming the equivalent of 'R18' videos into the UK. The Home Office seem alive to this difficulty and seem prepared to take the necessary steps to combat it. Vigilance will be required, however, over the next few critical years.

Telephones

This sector of the industry has grown at a phenomenal rate since it first appeared in 1985. There are many legitimate services, and number prefixes like 0898 have become familiar to the public for needs as varied as finding out weather information, or voting in a TV opinion poll. But the three main types of 0898 services have all been exploited by pornographers.

With recorded messages you dial an advertised number and listen to a taped message usually spoken by a woman with much innuendo and sexual content; with one-on-one messages there is a live conversation with a woman paid by a company to keep men talking for as long as possible often by 'talking dirty'; and with chatlines you are linked for conversation with a number of other callers you did not previously know.

The way the system works is that commercial companies lease lines from British Telecom, install the necessary equipment, and British Telecom agree to pay the companies a proportion of the income of each call made by individuals. The calls are expensive, almost equivalent to the cost of calling a European country. There has been an ongoing battle to try and restrict these services because of the content and because of the impact that the high charges have. Calls are often made by people other than the telephone subscriber who pays the bill, eg young people and employees who telephone during work time. Cases have been known of quarterly bills of £3,000 or £4,000. A bill of £500 when the normal usage would be £70 or £80 is not unusual. Like other forms of pornography individuals become addicted. One case involved a young man whose parents successfully barred him from using their own telephone when they discovered the problem. He then started using a telephone in a church office. When that was discovered he bought himself a telephone unit which he could plug in to other people's telephone sockets when he got the chance.

Terry Lewis MP has led a tireless campaign to have greater restrictions introduced on these services. The authorities seem to have had largely deaf ears. They rely on a non-statutory regulating committee (ICSTIS—the Independent Committee for the Supervision of Telephone Information Services) which has been of limited effect. Any doubts about the scale of this problem are dispelled by a quick glance at the many pages of advertisements in *The Sport* newspaper. British Telecom has introduced a scheme to enable individual subscribers to bar the calling of certain numbers from their telephones. This is a partial answer, but the problems of advertising and content remain.

Computers

Another area of concern is the development of computers in communicating pornographic images. The relatively innocent format of a computer game has been adapted to include scenarios like chasing after naked women before attacking them, or gradually revealing female sexual parts in more and more detail. This is an issue which individuals can effectively combat by complaining to specific magazines that advertise the games, or, where they are sold through computer-user groups, by arguing strongly that the materials should be deleted from catalogues.

The quality of computer graphics is improving all the time and at the most advanced level the imagery is as powerful as photographs. The computer has also been used as a means of communication between individuals interested in a particular kind of material, eg paedophilia.

Distribution outlets

The main kinds of distribution outlets for pornography in the UK are:

Ordinary shops

'Soft' pornography is available in newsagents, video shops and other retailers who sell magazines, books, newspapers or videos. Thousands of shops are involved in this way in the United Kingdom.

Mail order

The mail-order business has assumed increasing importance in recent years. A number of the main pornography companies are aggressively marketing their products through direct mail. CARE has frequently received complaints from individuals who have received catalogues through the post advertising pornographic videos or other material. It seems that the pornography companies will buy mailing lists in the same way as other selling organisations. Mail order is also used for the sale of more explicit illegal materials advertised in pornographic magazines. Foreign suppliers see it as a safer way of sending material into the UK than using couriers or ordinary freight. Small individual packages are difficult to detect and stop.

Sex shops

There are about 100 of these shops in England and Wales selling sex articles including all kinds of pornography. They sell the 'harder' kind of material and although they have to comply with the law on content, convictions have been secured for selling material that is illegal.

Technology

Increasingly pornography can be purchased directly in the home through new technical media like satellite television, telephones and computers. These media forms can be more difficult to regulate and they seem assured of continuing growth.

Trends in the industry

The main trends that can be identified in the pornography industry are:

The exploitation of more media and more sophisticated distribution systems

One hundred and fifty years ago the only forms of pornography available would have been written text, printed drawings or the theatre. Now, as new forms of media have become available, the pornographers have not been slow to capitalise on the opportunities they offer. Paul's words in Romans 1:30 come to mind: 'Men invent ways of doing evil.'

The achievement of greater sales

It is not easy to get information about the sales of pornography. Some observers have suggested that the sales of pornographic magazines are falling. For example, the Home Office review of pornography effects by Cumberbatch and Howitt in 1990 used readership survey figures suggesting a decline in readership of six top titles from 5.5 million in 1984 to 3.3 million in 1988.[14] Such figures need to be treated with great caution. Undertaking readership surveys or estimating circulation figures of pornographic magazines is an entirely different exercise from seeking such figures for other kinds of magazines. In the latter case, the publishers are keen to co-operate, giving accurate figures, and readers have few qualms about providing indications of who else reads their magazines. Pornography publishers are not like a conventional business and at different times will have reasons for either boosting or reducing their figures.

Furthermore, as we have seen, there has been a growth in the kinds of media available and forms of pornography sold. The evidence suggests that the size of the market as a whole has grown, as have individual sectors. In the case of magazines, the fact that there are far more titles available means that while some of the main magazines may have suffered a small reduction in sales, this has been taken up by other less well-known titles.

A few years ago CARE was contacted by a wholesaler dealing with newspapers and magazines. He wanted to help provide some information for our pornography campaign. He personally tried to restrict the number of magazines he sold, even though there was pressure from publishers to carry more titles. In the prosperous area of England

WHERE THERE'S MUCK THERE'S BRASS

in which he operated some of the leading pornographic magazines had sales figures equal to those of publications like *Horse and Hound* and *Homes and Gardens*, which were leading sellers in his area. Arguments may continue about the overall level of sales of pornography, but while individual magazine titles can sell half a million copies a month there is no reason to be complacent.

'Softer' material has become 'harder', and 'harder' material more extreme

The evidence for this comes both from academic research, which has looked at the content of pornography particularly in magazines and films, and from comments by those who monitor the trade. Malamuth and Spinner concluded that sexual violence in *Playboy* and *Penthouse* increased five-fold between 1973 and 1977.[15] Officers at Scotland Yard have personally relayed to me their concern that so-called 'soft' pornographic magazines are getting 'harder'. They express particular worries about the text accompanying pictures. The text is now much more explicit than ten years ago, and this often gets missed in quick analyses.

Greater integration of the industry

Pornography is big business and is dominated by a number of large networks of companies. The three most significant groups in the United Kingdom are those operated by David Sullivan, Adam Cole and Paul Raymond respectively. Sullivan's empire extends from newspapers through video production and distribution, to magazines, mail order, sex shops and telephone pornography. He uses a network of companies going under different names like Roldvale, Apollo, Conegate, Sheptonhurst, Darker Enterprises (there is actually a Mr Darker!), Quietlynn and others. In some of these companies Sullivan claims now to have no interest. Part of his difficulty is that he was convicted in 1982 of living off immoral earnings, ie prostitution, which means that he cannot personally apply for a licence for a sex shop as he could be turned down under the Act because of his conviction. Cole has made his money through the development of a video series called 'Electric Blue'. This has spawned the *Electric Blue* magazine and now 'Electric Blue' sex shops. Paul Raymond is best known for his 'Raymond Revue Bar' and for his company's production of magazines like *Men Only* and *Escort*.

For pornographers it makes commercial sense to own companies involved in different sectors of the pornography business. It ensures greater profits and greater security in a business where changes in regulation, eg on videos, can quickly reduce turnover. For example, if a pornographer owns both mail-order outlets and sex shops, losing business on one side can be compensated for by increasing business on the other. What this means is that in tackling the pornography problem in the UK campaigners need to be aware of the slippery beast they are dealing with, and its size and power. We must not take on our campaigns lightly and quite obviously must ensure that we have adequate spiritual protection for all that we do.

6

The 1959 Act And All That

From a practical standpoint we are now in a position where the law as it applies to magazines has become farcical.

This statement was not made by a member of an anti-pornography pressure group nor by an opposition MP, but by Superintendent Michael Hames, the Head of the Obscene Publications Squad at Scotland Yard. He was speaking at a fringe meeting organised jointly by CARE and the National Viewers' and Listeners' Association at the Conservative Party Conference in October 1990. Superintendent Hames is responsible for action by the Metropolitan Police against pornography and heads a team of officers at Scotland Yard. His forthrightness was prompted by long-standing difficulties with interpreting the 1959 Obscene Publications Act, thrown into sharp relief by a couple of recent cases.

The police submitted what they considered to be illegal pornographic material in a magazine called *Black Masters, White Slaves* before two juries—one in Wales and the other at Knightsbridge in London. The magazine contained explicit scenes of homosexual buggery, oral sex and bondage. Both juries found the magazines not obscene within the terms of the 1959 Act. This came after a decision by Nottingham City Magistrates that an edition of *Penthouse*, a magazine available in many newsagents, *was* obscene. It is not surprising that Superintendent Hames should conclude, 'Surely the time has come to draft an alternative which will enable us to be rather more certain about what is acceptable to the majority.'

The patchwork quilt

There is a 'patchwork quilt' of legal provisions in England and Wales which touch on some aspects of pornography. Scotland and Northern Ireland share some of these provisions but also have separate and distinctive statutes. Over this 'patchwork quilt' there also exists a single blanket law (in England and Wales) defining what is acceptable in terms of *content* of any media: the 1959 Obscene Publications Act. This is the most significant Act which so urgently needs amendment. But first we need to look at some of the 'patchwork quilt'.

Sex shops

These are restricted by a licensing procedure under the Local Government (Miscellaneous Provisions) Act 1982. Any shop selling to a 'significant degree' a range of 'sex articles' (terms defined in the Act in a less than precise way!) have to obtain a licence from a local authority. Licensed sex shops are the only retail outlets allowed to sell or hire the most explicit (R18) videos. (See pages 106-108 for further details on sex shop legislation and campaigning against such shops.)

Films

Under the Cinematograph Act 1909 local authorities have to licence any cinemas in their area and approve the films they show. In practice, virtually all authorities accept the advice of the British Board of Film Classification (which is not a statutory body but a self-regulating body appointed by the film industry) and will only show those films classified by the Board. Occasionally local authorities will take their own decisions. One example would be *The Last Temptation of Christ* where some authorities refused to allow it to be shown in their areas.

Videos

These come under the 1984 Video Recordings Act which established a system for certifying all videos and gave that task to the British Board of Film Classification. The Board do refuse certificates to a number of videos each year on grounds of violence or pornographic content and demand cuts in other videos before granting certificates. They produce a very interesting annual report which reviews trends in the industry.

Telephones

Section 43 of the Telecommunications Act 1984 re-enacted earlier provisions which made it illegal to use a public telephone system for communication of an 'indecent, obscene or menacing character'.

While occasional prosecutions are being made under this Act against individual obscene callers it has proved wholly ineffective in dealing with commercial telephone pornography and chatlines (see pages 65-67 above).

Broadcasting

The 1990 Broadcasting Act reiterated earlier provisions stressing the importance of standards of decency and taste on television and radio, and established the Broadcasting Standards Council to consider complaints about programmes offending these standards. It also brought broadcasting for the first time within the scope of the 1959 Obscene Publications Act (of which more below).

Child pornography

The 1978 Protection of Children Act, as amended by the Criminal Justice Act 1988, introduced specific offences concerning the distribution of indecent material relating to children and made possession of such material an offence.

Customs legislation

There is a separate body of legislation concerned with what it is legal to import into or export from the UK. The 1876 Customs Consolidation Act made it an offence to import 'indecent' material. 'Indecent' is a legal concept which catches more pornographic material than 'obscene'. It would for example in some cases include full frontal nudity, which would normally not be considered obscene. This difference has caused a problem with the European Community because the UK appeared to be imposing a higher moral standard on material being imported than on material manufactured and distributed in Britain. The European Court ruled in 1986 in an important case concerning the import of 'sex dolls' that the UK must apply the same test to imported and home-produced goods. Customs officers will now only seize imported material if they are confident it would be considered 'obscene' under the 1959 Act.

Legislation Controlling Display

The Indecent Displays (Control) Act 1981 restricts what can be *seen* in a *public* place. (The definition of indecent is the same as with the customs legislation mentioned above.) It therefore applies to the covers of magazines and videos, window displays and so on. Magazines or videos with indecent covers can only be displayed in an area where people under 18 cannot enter. Most sex shops therefore forbid access to children under 18, and some other shops have a separate partitioned area for more extreme material.

Mail Order

The Post Office Act 1953 restricts the sending of indecent material through the post. This section of the Act is now rarely used and the Post Office have no special staff dealing with intercepting indecent material.

Having read the last few pages perhaps you will understand why the analogy of a 'patchwork quilt' of provisions is appropriate. But overlying all this legislation stands one very important Act: the 1959 Obscene Publications Act.

The 1959 Obscene Publications Act

Section 1 of the 1959 Act defines whether an article should be considered 'obscene' in law. It is important to note that the word used is 'obscene' and not 'indecent' or 'pornographic'. The word pornography does not actually appear nor is defined in UK law. The 1959 'test' or definition of obscenity reads:

> (1) For the purposes of this Act an article shall be deemed to be obscene if its effect or (where the article comprises two or more distinct items) the effect of any one of its items is, if taken as a whole, such as to tend to deprave and corrupt persons who are likely, having regard to all relevant circumstances, to read, see or hear the matter contained or embodied in it.

This definition is not easy to understand or apply. A jury or magistrate considering allegedly obscene material presented by the police do not have to consider what they think of the material itself but what *impact* they think the material will have. This provides plenty of scope for lawyers to argue about whether the 'test' that an article is obscene has been proved. They can argue that the material was not designed to be seen by children and, because of warnings on its cover, would only be purchased by people over 18 who were unlikely to be 'depraved or corrupted' by the material.

They can put policemen in the witness box and

say 'Do you feel depraved and corrupted by this?'—a question that is very difficult for an individual to answer. If a hardened policeman says 'No—I've seen material like this before. I don't feel depraved or corrupted,' which might be a realistic response, material may be found *not* to be obscene. On the other hand, if he says, 'Yes, this material did "tend to deprave and corrupt me," ' it sounds as if he is a very weak character. Furthermore, the words 'deprave and corrupt' themselves represent very stringent language. Mr Justice Byrne, in the first case under the 1959 Act, the notorious *Lady Chatterley's Lover* case, said, ' "Deprave and corrupt" means to be morally bad, to pervert, or to debase and corrupt morally. It is extremely difficult to prove this.'

A further difficulty is the likely audience or readership of the material. The definition stresses that it applies to 'people who are likely, having regard to all relevant circumstances, to read, see or hear the matter contained or embodied therein.' This allows defendants to produce evidence that those likely to see the material are all adults well used to such pornography. For example, lawyers will say, 'It was on the top shelf out of the reach of children.' But such arguments, by concentrating on the likely *immediate* readership, ignore those who may later see the material. Books, magazines and videos may be seen by children in the street, on the rubbish dump, or in the home where the material has been taken after purchase. Material is often passed on from one individual to another. The law, however, only takes account of the immediate circumstances in which the material was being displayed and offered for sale.

Apart from the definition of obscenity, another problem concerns Section 4 of the 1959 Act, the so-called 'public good' defence. This Section allows someone who publishes an article which might otherwise be deemed obscene to defend its publication on the grounds that it is 'in the interest of science, literature, art or learning, or other objects of general concern.' There is also provision for the opinions of experts to be heard in a trial in order to testify to the artistic merit or otherwise of the material in question. In the *Lady Chatterley* case no less than 35 expert witnesses were called defending the artistic merit of the book.

The general concept of the 'public good' defence is not unreasonable. Of course it is right that some works of art which include nudity and medical text books dealing with sexual matters (to take just two examples) should be allowed. Difficulties arise however when this defence is exploited by lawyers (eg by suggesting pornographic magazines have therapeutic value for sex criminals) who have already attacked the weak central definition of obscenity.

Penalties under the 1959 Act

There are two possible penalties under the Act. The first is under Section 2 and involves trial by magistrate or jury and on conviction a fine or imprisonment. A Section 2 prosecution is brought by the police against publishers or distributors only in the case of the most extreme materials.

Such prosecutions are, however, fraught with problems. Trials are long and costly. The vagueness of the definition and the loopholes it provides for defence counsel mean there is no certainty a prosecution will be secured before a magistrate or jury. The police are therefore somewhat wary of bringing Section 2 prosecutions.

The alternative penalty is under Section 3 of the Act and permits the police to seize and forfeit obscene material. Those selling or distributing the material are not penalised other than by losing their stock. The police secure a warrant issued by a Justice of the Peace, seize the material they believe to be obscene, bring it before the JP who may issue a Summons to the occupier of the premises to appear before the Magistrates Court explaining why the articles should not be forfeited. If the court is satisfied the articles are obscene they order the articles to be forfeited and the police subsequently arrange for their destruction.

While this Section 3 penalty is easier to implement, and is less costly in police and court time, it lacks real bite. The problem is that if the material is seized and destroyed it is often not long before the shelves are restocked and the offending material is once again in circulation. Pornographers may simply republish the same contents in different covers, and so a cat and mouse game continues with the police. The police are faced with a dilemma: although Section 3 forfeiture proceedings do not provide an effective lasting penalty, they have tended to use them more than Section 2 prosecutions because of the problems with the definition of obscenity.

This brief discussion of the law reveals the inadequacies of the current situation. Not surprisingly retailers have little idea of what the law actually requires. The definition is so confused that they are not sure if what they are selling is legal or illegal. The law is even interpreted differently in different parts of the country.

It is perhaps helpful at this point to deal with one or two of the questions that are most often asked about the law:

Can pornography be sold to children under 18?

The answer is in many circumstances yes. There is a restriction that material with indecent covers should not be sold in a public place. As a result of this some specialist magazine shops have separate sections of their premises where children under 18 cannot go. This will include material that is somewhat more explicit than the usual fare of magazines found in newsagents. Children under 18 are also barred from sex shops. Videos with an '18' classification cannot legally be hired or sold to children under that age. But the fact remains that in newsagents' shops there is no statutory bar on the sale of pornographic magazines to children.

Must pornographic magazines be displayed on the top shelf?

This is a convention rather than a legal requirement. The idea is probably associated with cases under the Obscene Publications Act where the defence has argued that since the material was displayed on a top shelf it was less likely to be seen by children and therefore could not be held to 'deprave and corrupt' its potential audience. But there is no legal requirement for material to be so displayed.

How can the law be changed?

There have been a number of attempts over the years to change the 1959 Act. There are two broad categories of proposal:

(a) The amendment approach

This involves producing a new definition of obscenity but retaining the essential framework of the 1959 Act. The formula which has gained most currency is to replace 'a tendency to deprave and corrupt' with 'grossly offensive to a reasonable person'. The 'grossly offensive' definition would be linked to the manner in which the material portrays, deals with or relates to a short list of activities, for example acts of violence or cruelty, incidents of a horrific nature, sexual activity or genital organs, urinary or excretory functions.

This approach is one which has much to commend it because it fits into the traditions of British law. The concept of a 'reasonable person' is one which is well known. The definition also shifts the focus from the *impact* the material may have to the *content*. The definition does not remove all subjective judgement, but it appears to avoid some of the worst problems with the 1959 Act. Gerald Howarth MP put forward a bill broadly including this form of definition in 1987; it only failed to proceed because of the General Election in that year bringing an early end to the parliamentary session.

(b) The substitution approach

Some groups (including a number of feminist organisations) have argued that the Howarth approach does not go far enough and that the law needs to be entirely rewritten with a new definition of pornography. One model that has been suggested is creating a new offence of incitement to sexual hatred based on the parallel of race relations legislation where material is defined as illegal if it incites to racial hatred. While in theory the concept is appealing, sexual hatred is a more nebulous concept than racial hatred, and much more difficult to prove. Such a definition could simply lead to endless legal debates about whether the material really provoked 'sexual hatred' and what the term means.

Apart from these two main types of approach there have been other attempts to amend the law. Some have argued for a definitive list of types of material that would come under an umbrella definition of pornography something like 'the graphic sexually explicit subordination of women'. The problem with such an approach is similar to that which confronted Winston Churchill MP (grandson of the former Prime Minister) in 1986 when he produced a detailed list of activities which might be defined as obscene: it invites the pornographers to think of something which is not on the list and then claim that since it is not, it must be legal. The Howarth approach avoids this by a short list of general categories rather than a long list of specific acts.

Another approach, suggested by Dawn Primarolo MP, is to remove all pornography totally from the sale of general shops and limit it to shops with a specific licence. 'Pornography' is defined in a way to catch all 'soft' pornographic magazines. This is like extending the current sex shops legislation to enable a much broader range of materials.

As we shall see, the sex shop legislation is far from perfect as a model for more general restrictions on pornography. Some councils have refused to use the licensing procedure and in other areas the big pornography companies have managed through long legal battles to keep shops open. While it is appealing to think of an effective licensing procedure that would stop the sale of all pornographic magazines in newsagents and switch it to licensed premises, the danger is that it will actually increase the sales of pornography through concentrating it in specialist outlets. Furthermore, because it is such an extreme step it may prove impossible to enforce.

For completeness, mention must also be made of Clare Short's attempts to ban topless photographs from newspapers. This had a narrow purpose which did not affect the definition of obscenity, but is a move that CARE would support.

Conclusions

Changing the law is not easy but a way must be found to do so, bearing in mind the objectives of clarity, enforceability and consistency mentioned in Chapter 2. At this stage I believe that our efforts should be concentrated on an amendment to the definition of 'obscene' similar to that which Gerald Howarth MP proposed but with some attention paid to the definition to ensure that it fully takes account of the impact that pornography can have in degrading women. However, we should continue to consider other approaches to the problem on a longer-term basis. There may be scope for including some of the other ideas as they are refined over the course of the next few years. There is certainly a strong case for bringing together the patchwork of measures described in this chapter into a single Act dealing with pornography in all its different forms.

One of the most important issues is whether the police believe they can implement any change. Implementation will be helped by a general change in the climate towards pornography resulting from what individual members of the public think. The more that society as a whole is convinced that pornography is harmful and degrading, the more likely it is that juries and magistrates who are members of that society, whatever the weakness in legal definitions, will seek to enforce the law more rigorously. A changed definition and a changed attitude should secure a significant reduction in the sale of pornography.

7

The Special Horror of Child Pornography

The circumstances in which I first saw child pornography are etched on my memory. It was a clear summer's day in 1989. I had arranged to call on the Head of the Obscene Publications Squad at Scotland Yard with an American visitor. I had had to see quite a variety of pornography in the previous year as part of CARE's campaign, but nothing prepared me for what I saw that afternoon. The police officers showed us a variety of material selected from that retrieved in the course of their raids. The adult pornography was utterly degrading but not exceptional of its type. Then we saw a clip from a German-produced video circulating in this country of an altogether different order. It showed an 8-year-old girl being forced to engage in the most demeaning of sexual acts. I distinctly recall feeling ill at that point. The girl's look of bewilderment, anguish, fear and pain was unforgettable.

Child pornography is a distinct category of pornography. This book is mainly about the visual portrayal of the degradation of adult women. It would be wrong, however, not to mention the horrors of child pornography. In some ways the word 'pornography' is not adequate for this material. Child pornography is no less than a visual record of child abuse. Each video or photograph records a criminal offence against a child. All child pornography is illegal. Whereas there are those who seek to defend adult pornography, very few people in the UK would argue that the law on child pornography should be relaxed.

Members of the public can only have a limited role in combating child pornography. The police need our support especially to ensure that they have the necessary resources and political backing. CARE seeks to represent individual Christians in pressing the case with the Government that the fight against child pornography should be a priority. For the individual Christian the most important step we can take on child pornography is to pray. These few pages are intended to acquaint you with some of the background to enable you to pray more knowledgeably and therefore more effectively.

Why is child pornography produced?

It is hard to understand why men and women produce child pornography. The Obscene Publications Squad at Scotland Yard point to a number of reasons:

(a) Paedophiles (those people, usually men, who desire sexual relations with children) produce the material for their own sexual arousal. Long after the thrill of the initial abuse may have worn off it can be recreated in fantasy through looking at records of the material. Many paedophiles retain visual records of their abuse.

(b) Photographs and videos can be used to persuade children to take part in sexual acts. Some child abusers use adult pornography for this purpose, but child pornography can more easily entrap children who are told, 'Others do it—why shouldn't you?' It can also be used as a means of blackmailing the children once they are abused: 'Unless you keep quiet I'll show these pictures to your mummy or daddy.'

(c) Material is also used as a medium of exchange. The people involved in this dreadful addiction like to swop or pass on the visual records of abuse. (When the police track down a paedophile who has a collection of child pornography they often find an accompanying record keeping system. The investigating officers can trace the same photographs or videos through different parts of the network of contacts of that paedophile.)

Child pornography is sometimes sold for profit. It is probably true to say, however, that in recent years this sector has been less commercially exploited than adult pornography, because of the risks of being caught by the police. Money does change hands but often any gains are ploughed back into buying further child pornography, rather than as a commercial exercise per se. Widespread commercial activities seem to be confined to other countries like Holland and the Far East.

It should be clear from this that child pornography and child abuse are inextricably linked. (Of course there are many individual cases of child abuse that do not involve child pornography.) The particular horror of abuse involving a photographic record is that the child has no control over where the photographic record will end up. The photograph may be in existence throughout the child's lifetime and at some later date may return to haunt the abused, evoking memories of an evil carried out years before. The police sometimes find pictures of an individual child in a paedophile's collection which they have later been able to identify and trace to that individual now grown up. Often such a person can help expose the true extent of the paedophile's crime.

Profile of a paedophile

Our image of a paedophile as a dirty old man in a raincoat is sadly misplaced. Many are professional, middle-aged, middle-class individuals, some with a prominent position in the community. They tend to be extremely orderly individuals who maintain careful records of their collection. Often there will be diaries recording the transactions and exchanges they have made. Photographs will be carefully indexed and filed away.

This tendency to record-keeping often offers the police an enormous amount of evidence, much of which they do not have the resources to pursue. Scotland Yard is constantly faced with agonising decisions about which names they should investigate and what avenues of enquiry are most likely to bear fruit. They have been helped in this by a change in the law in 1988 which made possession of child pornography an offence. Previously evidence of distribution had to be produced for a prosecution to succeed under the Protection of Children Act or the Obscene Publications Act. CARE would like to see the law even further strengthened so that a person suspected of distributing child pornography can be immediately arrested and taken to a police station rather than merely summonsed to appear before a court at an appropriate time. Such a change would ensure that those involved in distributing child pornography do not have the opportunity immediately to contact their accomplices following a visit from the police. It would also enable finger-print evidence to be used in cases against child pornographers. Often this evidence is vital to demonstrate that the alleged distributor had actually handled the material. Changing the law takes time, but every justifiable addition to the police's armoury in fighting child pornography is worth campaigning for.

An international business

Child pornography is an international business. As the law has tightened in European countries and in the USA the production of material on any commercial scale has shifted to the Far East, in particular Thailand. There is evidence of trade in magazines and videos between individual European countries, the USA and the Far East. The police forces in these countries co-operate in dealing with such material and US officers have traced material back to producers in Thailand and successfully succeeded with the Thai authorities in prosecuting such individuals.

Links with the mainstream

Although child pornography is a special case we should recognise that there are links between this kind of pornography and the mainstream which should be of particular concern:

Advertisements

Classified advertisements in mainstream pornographic magazines and even magazines like *Exchange & Mart* have been used by paedophiles as outlets for their material. The police watch such magazines carefully and follow up on advertisements which contain tell-tale code words like 'younger material' or 'lolitas'. An exposé by the BBC2 *Newsnight* team of the use of *Exchange & Mart* in January 1990 was followed up by a CARE-affiliated group in Portsmouth with the Directors of that publication. After correspondence from the Portsmouth group they promised not to include any advertisements of this type in the future, thus preventing their magazine from becoming an outlet for visual child abuse.

Simulated child pornography

In their quest for new ways of making money pornographers have seen that there is a market for material which purports to be photographs of young girls or have some of the characteristics of such girls, eg genitalia without pubic hair. There is a genre of magazine known as 'shaver material' featuring this phenomenon which bridges the gap between adult and child pornography. Often such magazines also include pictures showing sequences with girls in school uniform.

Addiction

Adult pornography is a gateway to child pornography. Paedophilia has no single cause which therapists and psychiatrists can point to with absolute certainty. In some cases one factor is a general addiction to pornography which then becomes focused in a desire for photographs of children. This is part of the escalator effect to which Dr Victor Cline refers (see Chapter 3) where some men start with mainstream pornography and move increasingly into bizarre material.

These linkages mean that action against adult pornography does have some bearing on child pornography. Of course, it is essential that the police and customs officials should maintain their high level of action directly against child pornography. But we the general public must guard against the seepage of this material into the mainstream, or the use of mainstream materials as a means of contact for those seeking child pornography.

8

A Practical Response

'I just did not realise what was in the magazines. I sold them because I could make good money from them. But now I know what they contain I don't want to sell them any more.'

That was what a Bristol newsagent said following a campaign by a local CARE Core Group. Since 1988 that reaction has been repeated throughout the UK as local groups of Christians have come together to campaign against the continuing sale of pornographic magazines in their neighbourhood. It has been a low-key campaign attracting considerable local publicity but not seeking the limelight of national press or television coverage. I hope by this stage of reading about pornography you will be convinced that you want to do something about it. This chapter sets out a number of areas where you can make a contribution.

An attitude of non-acceptance

Our society has grown to accept pornography. The

response of Christians has differed little from that of society as a whole. Most of us have become proficient at being armchair activists. We sit there, reading our newspapers, watching the television and occasionally shaking our heads and tut-tutting at some new horror story. Invariably we say, 'Somebody should do something about this.' In the case of the sale of pornography the stakes are high. Its mass availability ensures mass impact. If we do nothing the risk is that those who purchase pornography will feel comfortable with what they are doing and believe that the sexual activities portrayed in pornographic magazines are what most people think sex is like. For some men (as we have seen in Chapter 3) the mass sale of pornography begins to justify in their own minds the actions that they later take. They think, 'If the local newsagent sells pictures of naked women in provocative sexual poses, then surely the people that go into that shop condone the sale, and the women are inviting sexual attack.'

That is an extreme portrayal of the mindset of some men. Understanding the impact the sale of pornography can have should not, however, drive us to a response motivated by guilt and ill-directed anger (see pages 54-56 above). Rather it should convince us of the importance of carefully thought-out action. We need first to attune ourselves not to accept things that we have come to accept without thinking. In the words of Romans 12:2 we need to ensure we are not being 'conformed to this world' but are being transformed by the renewing of our minds. This does not mean a 'holier-than-thou' attitude of self-righteousness, but a prayerful concern to persuade others not to accept pornography.

Emphasising the positive

Some identify campaigning against pornography with a negative spoilsport image: 'It's the Victorian prudes at it again.' There is a grain of truth in such criticism. Christians have in the past been quick to condemn others for sexual impropriety without offering a positive joyful alternative. That is why this book starts with a chapter headed 'Sex Was God's Idea'. Positive action by the church to present sexual relationships in the proper context plays a vital role in campaigning against the false images of pornography. But our positive attitude can go further. We should not just campaign against what is bad but applaud what is good. We should support newsagents who do not stock pornography. A central feature of CARE's *Picking Up the Pieces* campaign is the awarding of a sticker 'We've said NO to Porn—Family Shop'. We should congratulate newspapers that don't take advertisements for telephone-message services. We should write to television and radio producers commending the programmes we enjoy that do not include smut and sexual innuendo. A Christian approach to campaigning should have as key words in any glossary of terms: 'thank you'.

The immediate response

Practical action against pornography can be divided into the immediate and the planned. Sometimes we need to make an immediate response to things that we see and hear. If we do not make a quick response the opportunity will pass and the impact will either lessen or be irrelevant if we attempt to take action later. This is made clearer by example:

(a) You are on holiday staying on a campsite. The shop on the site which is frequented by all the children to buy sweets, comics, and so on, stocks twenty pornographic magazines prominently displayed. In such a situation you have a choice. It is easy to think, 'Well, I'm on holiday, I don't want to disrupt things with the campsite. I want an easy life. It's sad but that's the way things are.' An alternative reaction would be to take the opportunity to speak to the owner, perhaps when settling your bill. You can say how much you have enjoyed your stay, commend them on the good things on the site, and then explain how sorry you were that he or she had chosen to sell such a range of pornographic magazines.

(b) You are on a business trip and stay overnight at a hotel which you may not visit again. You discover that of the films on offer on the hotel's entertainment system half are of a sexually explicit nature. Unless you react while you are at the hotel the opportunity will be lost. No one will know what you felt. What you can do is complain to the hotel management, and perhaps follow it up with a letter to the hotel company's head office.

(c) You see a TV programme that you thoroughly enjoy except that it is spoilt by a sexual scene unrelated to the plot. The opportunity is there to write or telephone the television station congratulating them on their programme but expressing your disappointment at the scene in question.

In all these examples the likelihood is that if you say, 'I must do something about that tomorrow,' it will not get done. It is the immediacy of the response that is telling. You saw it, you did not like it and you reacted. Such a response does not need to be harsh, although sometimes it is helpful to show our anger. There is plenty of opportunity in these situations for positive commendation.

A few years ago I had to make a long journey from Scotland to London and back again, which involved driving the entire length of the M6 and M1 stopping frequently at motorway service stations. The difference between the shops of two of the main rival service station operators was striking. One company had no pornographic magazines available for sale. The other had. My response was to write to the Chairman of the company with the no-pornography policy congratulating them on their stance and explaining how much I had enjoyed using their facilities. I also wrote to the other company expressing my disappointment, and saying that, wherever possible, I would only use the facilities of their competitors which did not stock pornography.

Such immediate reactions do not always come easily to us. Often incidents happen at inconvenient times when we are busy, rushing to an appointment, or relaxing on holiday, when we don't want to get involved. But we can train ourselves to deal with such incidents quickly and easily and without getting them out of proportion. We can make comments to those we meet without going over the top or letting the incident spoil our day. The key to this is practice and a prayerful response to react with love, grace and righteous anger in different situations. God will supply us with the appropriate self-confidence.

A planned response

There are other situations where immediate responses may well be unhelpful and fail to achieve the purpose we want. It would be counter-productive if those reading this book were immediately to dash into their local newsagents complaining about the top-shelf display. When you live in an area an immediate response is not essential. You will still live there tomorrow and the magazines will still be there tomorrow. A planned response is both more appropriate and more effec-tive. It also gives an opportunity to think through the repercussions of your action. Ask yourself a few questions. If you have been taking your news-papers from a particular newsagent for five years and he stocks twenty pornographic magazines, do you now intend to switch your trade to another newsagent if you cannot achieve a change in pol-icy? Are you prepared to go along with the incon-venience that may result? Are you prepared to convince others of your actions? It is wise to 'count the cost before building your tower' (Luke 14:28–30).

CARE's *Picking Up the Pieces* action pack was designed to meet these needs. It provides all the resources necessary to mount a carefully planned campaign against pornography. You can order the pack from CARE at the address at the back of this book. The main steps involved in the campaign, which can be adjusted to individual circumstances, are:

1. Preparation

Get together a team of six to ten people. Ideally these should be a mix of men and women from a variety of local churches in the area that you are targeting. If there is not already interest in the subject it is a good idea to contact local ministers and arrange to speak, eg at a spot in a service, in a women's meeting or even at one or two home groups. The team should meet together a few times before undertaking action and should especially pay attention to praying through the steps that they are going to take. Someone should be appointed to look after relations with the local press and someone else to look after a questionnaire (see Appendix A). Different team members can research different aspects of the problem and then share their research with others. For example, one could prepare a five-minute talk on the harm caused by pornography, another on the biblical basis of our concern, and a third on the law. Such preparation will give confidence and help in informing others. It is often surprising how little people (including newsagents) and others know about the problems pornography can cause and the legal framework within which they sell it.

2. Planning

This will involve selecting a number of newsagents that are centrally located in the area that you choose and frequented by members of your team and the churches they represent. (Five to ten newsagents is probably best for an initial campaign.) A questionnaire should be prepared that can be used in the local High Street or shopping precinct to ask about women's attitudes to pornography. A sample questionnaire is given in Appendix A—you can adapt questions to suit your own needs. A timetable should be established to attract maximum local media attention. This usually works best if you adopt a two-week intense period of activity. At the end of one week newsagents are visited explaining your group's concern about pornography (see step 3 below). On the following Monday or Tuesday (depending on the local editorial deadlines) a news release is issued to the local press and radio stations advising about the campaign and the questionnaire to be undertaken the following weekend. On the Monday afterwards a further press release is issued giving the results of the questionnaire. Experience has shown that following a timetable like this creates something of a local bandwagon of interest and increases the pressure on local retailers to respond.

3. Initial visit to newsagent

It is very important to get the campaign off on the right foot by having a successful visit to the newsagents you have targeted. This is best undertaken by two people, perhaps a man and a woman, at a time when the shops are not busy. This will vary, depending on the local area, but often mid-morning or early afternoon are good times, especially during school term. The purpose of the visit is to acquaint the newsagent with your campaign, explain your concern about their sale of pornography, and invite them to think about their policy. With larger shops, eg the chains like W H Smith and Menzies, it is important to speak to the shop manager rather than just an assistant. The visit is often made more effective by writing beforehand saying that you will be calling. This will demonstrate the seriousness with which you are approaching the issue.

It is good to have some information with which to provide the newsagent about pornography. The CARE action pack includes a leaflet about the impact of pornography and a card addressed to newsagents thanking them for the service they provide but encouraging them to change their policy on this one issue.

The visit must not be threatening. It should be clear that the campaign is not against newsagents but against pornography. One successful tactic if a newsagent is claiming that the material is harmless is to remove a magazine from the shelves and suggest that he reads an article accompanying a set of pictures. One young mum said to a newsagent, 'My children keep asking me why those magazines have ladies with no clothes on on the front. How should I answer them?' In another case a customer knew the newsagent well and that he had a 16-year-old daughter. She asked the newsagent whether he had thought about the reading material that the boys of his daughter's age were looking at. The point was pressed home with the question, 'Would you like your daughter's boyfriend to buy such material the day that he took your daughter out for her first date?' The newsagent changed his practice.

None of these tactics can be used indiscriminately but they do demonstrate that engaging the newsagent in conversation and getting him to think about what he is doing can lead to a change.

4. *The questionnaire*

Local newsagents or other sellers of pornography often hide behind the notion that no one minds it being sold. In one sense they are right, because people have not protested. Undertaking a questionnaire is a good way of finding out what local people think. It is best to include questions that have yes/no answers and experience suggests it may be most effective to have women questioning women about their attitudes. This is because women are those who are most directly affected by pornography.

Aim to question at least 300 people. The questionnaire is an opportunity to involve other women not on the main team; they too will probably come from local churches. The purpose is not to engage in long conversations with those questioned, rather, in a friendly and non-threatening way, to ask other women to express their views. The answers to the questions should be processed as quickly as possible after the survey has been completed. A further news release can then be issued to the local media for the next issue of the paper or a discussion programme on local radio.

5. *Follow-up*

When the questionnaire is completed newsagents can be sent the results and visited again to encourage them to change their minds. For those who do, or those who did not stock pornography in the first place, it is good to have some means of recognising their stance. It is possible to print a simple certificate linked to your local area conveying some sort of award for being a 'porn-free' newsagent. Another approach is to offer a sticker which can be put on the front window. Stocks of these stickers are included in CARE's action pack. Presenting such a certificate or sticker provides another media opportunity and you can even ask a local personality to perform the ceremony. MPs are often willing to do this because of the publicity they get, and that helps cement relationships between a local group and their Member of Parliament. Having established the group's credibility through the initial campaign it is possible then to tackle other newsagents outside the immediate area. It may not be necessary to undertake the questionnaire again, but each newsagent should be visited and encouraged to change his or her practice.

Campaigns like this have led on to other initiatives. In one area of Belfast all the local churches agreed to have a Sunday when they publicised and supported a local campaign and prayed against the impact of pornography. In Cheshire the success of the campaign was brought to the attention of the local Council and the councillors instructed the Trading Standards Department to write to all newsagents encouraging them not to stock pornography. While the Council's action had no legal sanction it was important in conveying the concern of public representatives on this issue. That action has now been repeated in other council areas in the North West of England and is something CARE will be encouraging as a national strategy. Wirral Metropolitan borough have actually introduced their own 'Porn-free Newsagents' scheme, including window display stickers, monitored by trading standards department staff.

It is entirely possible to alter the newsagents campaign and focus on another form of pornography, like videos. The Video Retailers Association have an excellent Family Code initiative to encourage retailers to concentrate on family-type videos rather than the more violent or sexual content of some '18' classified videos. A local group could join together with some video retailers to publicise this code and encourage the support of the responsible shops.

Another initiative which most definitely falls in the category of a planned response to pornography is campaigning for the closure of a local sex shop. Since 1982 sex shops have been subject to formal licensing by local councils. A survey by CARE in 1989 revealed that there were still some 100 sex shops throughout England and Wales. Planning and perseverance are the keys to success in closing down a sex shop. Each year the licence comes up for renewal and it has been firmly established in law that a council can change its mind and decide to turn down a licence previously granted even for some years.

What a local group must focus on is the grounds in law on which a licence can be refused. The two key factors are whether the operators have a criminal record or whether the local environment in which the shop is situated is unsuitable. Often such licences are renewed each year virtually on the nod. Any local group can, however, protest to the council. The most successful campaigns are those that have focused on establishing that the local area was unsuitable for the sex shop.

It is essential to make a written presentation with all the evidence that can be collected. This might include a map showing the location and pointing out local schools and churches and other community buildings; a survey of what local residents think about the location of the sex shop; a survey showing the number of women and children passing the shop on a typical day; and a statement setting out the views of the group.

Individual letters or a petition can help, but it is important that these do not concentrate on the moral aspect of pornography as the legislation does not allow that to be taken into account in decisions by the council. A letter which says, 'I think that the location of the sex shop at 24 Porn Lane is highly unsuitable because it is close to local schools and my house,' is worth far more than a letter saying pornography is evil, wicked and condemned in the Bible.

Often such battles are not won at the first round. Sex-shop owners have a lot to lose commercially if their licence is withdrawn and will often campaign through the courts to overturn decisions. Only a change in the law to prevent a shop trading during appeal proceedings will ultimately avoid such legal games. In the meantime, local people have often succeeded through sheer determination and perseverance in provoking councils to take all the necessary legal steps they can to get a shop to close.

One final point about campaigning. I am often asked whether Christians should get involved in campaigns organised by others, for example feminist groups, who are similarly seeking to remove pornography from the shelves of newsagents. My answer is usually 'yes'. Such groups often welcome support from individual Christians as long as it is clear those Christians are not trying to take the campaign over or to turn it into a Christian campaign. After all, if the boot were on the other foot, we would not welcome feminists hijacking our campaigns. It does mean working with individuals who hold very different views on other issues. But that is the nature of political action and not something we should worry about as long as it is clear that it is a single-issue campaign. By getting involved in attempts to remove pornography from newsagents it should be clear that you are not condoning action in support of abortion or of homosexual rights.

CARE works very successfully at a national level with groups and Members of Parliament who hold very different views on other issues which are important to us. Sometimes we have found that these groups are happy to have a private relationship with us but do not wish it to become too public. That is because they fear attack from libertarian groups who want to portray the anti-pornography campaign as a 'right-wing church campaign'. Such accusations are far wide of the target because CARE is a non-party political organisation which works with all parties. Moreover, our supporters to not come from one party. We just have to be prepared to work with such difficulties and extend friendship to those who find it awkward to reciprocate publicly for whatever reason. To fight against pornography is too big to let petty concerns intervene, as long as we Christians are able to walk with integrity, knowing that our actions before God are right and loving.

9

Help for the Addict

People buy books for different reasons. Some may have bought this book because they recognise the evil of pornography and want to learn how to campaign more effectively against it. Others may have been intrigued by the title and curious to find out more. Or you may be reading this because you are fascinated by the subject of pornography. Indeed you may be a consumer of it and have been wondering whether there is any hope that you may change. This chapter is for you. Be assured you can change with God's help and that of Christians around you.

The advice below is aimed at Christians but may be useful to other readers as well. We should not be surprised that some Christian men (and some women too) have a problem with pornography. After all, we are human and are tempted in the same way as everyone else. Sometimes the problem will develop long before someone becomes a Christian. For others it is something that happens much later when they have already made a Christian commitment. In either case the problem can be exacerbated by an enormous sense of guilt and shame. Pornography may bring temporary pleasure and excitement, but that does not compare with the long-term damage that it can do.

Five steps to freedom

It is vital to face up to the problem and seek help in resolving it. Although other people can help we must remember that above all else it is God's power that releases us from the grip of evil. My experience suggests that a step-by-step approach will secure freedom from this addiction. In many ways these steps are similar to those which bring release from other problems, like alcohol. They do need to be adapted to individual cases. For some people the problem will go away immediately (with relatively little struggle thereafter) if these steps are followed. For others it will take longer—but it is worth the fight:

1. Recognise the deceit

Friends who have struggled with pornography have invariably wanted to hide the problem. They are not proud of their addiction and do not find it easy to talk about. They have also wanted to hide the individual instances where they have bought or borrowed pornography and looked at it. They have gone to elaborate precautions to avoid people close to them finding out what they are doing. Magazines or videos are kept at work or only purchased on business trips. Some men even get to the stage of convincing themselves that what they are doing is right, that they have a need for such material but that it is best kept secret. Such attitudes inevitably lead to other problems especially the lying that is necessary to hide the truth. Deceit can become a major aspect of the problem.

2. Be honest

The most effective antidote to deceit is to be honest with yourself, with God, and with someone that you trust. The place to start is confessing your problem in the context of your own prayer time. I strongly recommend that you then arrange to see some men you trust: close Christian friends, or people who have pastoral responsibility for you (perhaps your vicar, minister, or house-group leader). Together you can constitute a small support group. There will be a strong temptation to hide some of the details. You may want to understate the extent of the material that you have been purchasing or the length of time that the problem has gone on. You may not want to reveal other sexual problems associated with your purchase of pornography, perhaps sexual liaisons with other women, or prostitution. However, it is vital to be entirely open and honest so that there is no backlog or hidden reservoir of mistakes that can lead to a sense of further condemnation later on. Bring everything into the light.

3. Repentance

There is an enormous release that comes from being honest about one's mistakes and sin. No individual action can take us outside of the love and grace of God. The next step which your support group can help you with is to repent. That means not only asking God for forgiveness for what has gone wrong but turning away from it, looking to the future and committing yourself not to make the same mistakes again. In the context of talking and praying through the problem it may be that you or your pastor will discern other factors at work in your difficulty. There may be a need for some counselling in your relations with women generally or, if you are married, with your wife. It is also possible that you will realise that there is some spiritual bondage involved in your addiction. The evil influence of pornography can trap some men in ways that devastate their growth as people. For some men release will only come through realising the directly spiritual nature of the attack and deliverance from it. A time of prayer and repentance with your support group is the right time and place to deal with such an issue if it is there.

4. *Agreeing to be accountable*

Repentance deals with the past and sets the scene for the future. But further steps are necessary to lay a good foundation for living a life free from an addiction to pornography. A top priority is to agree with your support group that you will be accountable to them as to how you cope with your previous problem. This can be a very simple arrangement whereby on a regular basis, perhaps weekly at first and then monthly, you will report how you are getting on and give them the right to call you and see how things are going. Such accountability can be of immeasurable value as you face temptation in the future. It is very helpful to call people at times when you feel you will be particularly tempted, eg a business trip, and ask for their prayer and support knowing that they will ask you how you got on afterwards. Doing this again tackles the root of the deceit inherent in pornography and can be very effective.

5. A strategy of avoidance

People who buy pornography develop habits in their consumption. There are particular times and places when they are most likely to buy the material and then look at it. It is therefore a good idea to take steps to avoid succumbing to the temptation at those times and places. (As 1 Corinthians 10:13 says, 'When you are tempted God will also provide a way out so that you can stand up under it.') It may mean going to a different newsagent, avoiding staying in a particular hotel, or indeed avoiding business trips altogether for a period. If pornography has consumed a major element of time and money it may be helpful to find an alternative outlet or hobby which is constructive rather than destructive. Much will depend on the individual likes and dislikes of the person concerned, and again the help of friends can be invaluable in such choices.

These steps form a basic framework and cannot encompass the needs of everyone. For some, medical or psychiatric help may be necessary and the discerning pastor will recognise this. For some married men where pornography has been introduced into the sexual relationship it is obvious that the wife will also need sensitive help and that the couple together may require counselling to reorder their sexual relationship.

Prevention is better than cure

Addiction to pornography can start for all sorts of reasons. Parents and youth leaders should recognise that they can help young people, especially boys, to avoid an addiction to pornography. This involves being willing openly to broach the subject of sexual relationships and how pornography falsely portrays them. Through developing a healthy openness we can help young men to avoid becoming trapped.

That brings this book full circle. Sex was and is God's idea. Pornography is a false image of the true nature of men and women as God created us. Let us celebrate the positive and campaign against the negative with all our might. Pornography has no part in God's new kingdom. It will be utterly destroyed with all the other evil influences in this world today. We therefore respond with confidence and humility to the challenge of expressing the true image of sex that God intended and combating the false image portrayed in pornography.

Appendix A

Questions

1. Are you aware that 'soft' porn magazines are sold in local newsagents? (eg *Men Only, Playboy, Penthouse, Fiesta, Knave, Escort,* etc)
2. Do you think the display of these magazines on the shelves is offensive?
3. Do you think such magazines cheapen women generally?
4. Do you think there is a link between pornographic magazines and the sexual and physical abuse of women?
5. Do you think these magazines encourage young people to treat sexual relationships casually?
6. Would you prefer that your local newsagents voluntarily stopped selling such magazines?
7. Would you be in favour of a legal ban on newsagents selling such material? (ie restricted to registered sex shops, or not at all)
8. Any other comment? (not necessary)

(14-20, 21-30, 31-40, 41-50, 51-60, 60+)

Q1	Q2	Q3	Q4	Q5	Q6	Q7	Q8	Age Range

√ Yes   Date: _____   Interviewer: _____
x No
? Don't know   Location: _____

117

Appendix B

USEFUL ADDRESSES

For information on campaigning against pornography from a Christian perspective, CARE will be delighted to help. The address to write to is: 53 Romney Street, London SW1P 3RF.

For specific information and support in relation to monitoring television the best source of advice is:

National Viewers' and Listeners' Association
Ardleigh
Colchester
Essex
CO7 7RH   Tel: 0206 230123

One other body with a general concern about pornography which has done some good work especially on telephone chatlines is:

National Council for Christian Standards in Society
65 Warwick Square
London
SW1V 2AL   Tel: 071-630 6162

There are a number of groups which have sprung up in recent years dealing with pornography from a feminist or 'civil liberties' perspective. The main groups are:

Campaign Against Pornography
The Unity Club
96 Dalston Lane
London
E8 1NG   Tel: 071-923 4303

Campaign against Pornography and Censorship
PO Box 844
London
SE5 9QP   Tel: 071-274 3072

Campaign for Press and Broadcasting Freedom
96 Dalston Lane
London
E8 1NG

Official Bodies/Trade Associations

Official bodies with a responsibility to monitor different aspects of pornography are:

The Broadcasting Standards Council, which monitors standards of taste and decency in television and will investigate complaints. Their address is:

Broadcasting Standards Council
5-8 The Sanctuary
London
SW1P 3JS   Tel: 071-233 0544

The British Board of Film Classification, is a trade association of the film industry which certifies all films shown in the UK. It also has a statutory responsibility for classifying video films sold or hired in the UK. They produce a very useful Annual Report reflecting on trends in the industry. Their address is:

British Board of Film Classification
3 Soho Square
London
W1   Tel: 071-439 7961

The Independent Committee for the Supervision of Standards of Telephone Information Services (ICSTIS), a body set up by British Telecom to monitor Chatlines and Telephone Information Services. They have produced a Code of Practice and will investigate complaints about individual lines. Their address is:

The Secretariat
ICSTIS
67-69 Whitfield Street
London
W1P 5RL   Tel: 071-636 6577
                 Complaints Line: 0800 500212

The Video Trade Association, a trade association of shops which specialise in selling or hiring videos. They have produced the idea of the 'Family Code'. Further information is available from them at:

Video Trade Association
54D High Street
Northwood
Middlesex
HA6 1BL   Tel: 09274 29122

If you receive something through the post that is of a pornographic or distasteful nature you can complain to the Direct Mail Services Standards Board at:

26 Eccleston Street
London
SW1W 9PY   Tel: 071-824 8651

To complain about bad taste or indecency in press articles write to the Press Complaints Commission at:

1 Salisbury Square
London
EC4

If you are concerned about advertising contact:

Advertising Standards Authority
Brook House
2-16 Torrington Place
London
WC1E 7HN   Tel: 071-580 5555

Appendix C

FURTHER READING

There is a limited amount of literature readily available in the UK providing a serious commentary on the issue of pornography. A very helpful book, currently out of print, is that by John Court, *Pornography: A Christian Critique* published by Paternoster Press Ltd. It may be available from second-hand sources, or some bookshops.

CARE has produced a number of resources dealing with the issue, available by mail order from 53 Romney Street, London SW1P 3RF:

Fatal Addiction (video), an interview between Dr James Dobson and Ted Bundy on the evening before Bundy's execution in America.

Picking Up the Pieces (action pack).

Parliament in the 1960s (CARE Booklet No. 7) by Jane Mellor

The Impact of Pornography (CARE Leaflet)

CARE Briefing Papers:
    SP1   *In Defence of Human Dignity*
    SP2   *Pornography—Evidence of its Harm*
    BP14 *Monitoring Your Local Video Supplier*
    BP16 *The Bible and Human Sexuality*

BP27 *Pornographic Phone Message Services*
BP37 *How the Media Can Help You*

Does pornography cause harm?

For those wishing to investigate more fully the question of the harm caused by pornography I recommend you read two contrasting official reports on the subject:

Pornography: Impacts and Influences—commissioned by the Home Office Research and Planning Unit (1990).
Can be purchased but available only from the Home Office Library.

Final Report of The Attorney General's Commission on Pornography (1986) published by Rutledge Hill Press.
Available from libraries.

A commentary on research and on other issues associated with the pornography problem is given in Catherine Itzin's book, *The Case Against Pornography: Sex Discrimination, Sexual Violence and Civil Liberties* (Oxford University Press, 1991).

A collection of the most recent research has been published in book form as *Pornography: Research Advances and Policy Considerations*, edited by Dolf Zillmann and Jennings Bryant (Lawrence Erlbaum Associates, 1989).
Available from libraries.

For personal testimony on the impact of pornography I would recommend the *Fatal Addiction* video of Ted Bundy's interview mentioned above under

CARE resources. It is also helpful to look at the book by Ron Sims which describes his own battle with pornography as complemented by his wife's account, *Flying Free* by Ron Sims, and *Looking for Love* by Maureen Sims, both published by Marshalls.

For further commentary on the special horror of child pornography the most authoritative work available is *Child Pornography* by Tim Tate (Methuen 1990).

For those wanting further insight into fighting the addiction of pornography, especially as it compares with other addictions, a useful short handbook is *Kicking It* by David Partington, Frameworks (1991).

Notes

1. Clare Short, *Dear Clare...* Hutchinson Radius 1991).

2. John and Janet Houghton, *A Touch of Love* (Kingsway Publications, 1986); Ed and Gaye Wheat, *Intended for Pleasure* (Scripture Union, 1979).

3. *Final Report of the Attorney General's Commission on Pornography (Commissioner Statements)*, (Rutledge Hill Press 1986) page 489.

4. Unpublished transcript available from CARE, 53 Romney Street, London SW1P 3RF.

5. Victor Cline, *Pornography Effects: Empirical Evidence* (unpublished).

6. W. L. Marshall 'Pornography and Sex Offenders' in *Pornography: Research Advances and Policy Considerations* edited by Dolf Zillman and Jennings Bryant (Laurence Erlbaum Associates 1989).

7. See John Court, *Pornography: A Christian Critique* (InterVarsity Press 1980).

8. This information was communicated to me by Alan Sears, former Executive Director of the Attorney General's Commission on Pornography.

9. See Dolf Zillman and Jennings Bryant, *Pornography: Research Advances and Policy Considerations* (Laurence Erlbaum Associates) *op cit.*

10. For a fuller assessment of the academic and other evidence of harm caused by pornography, see Catherine Itzin, *The Case Against Pornography: Sex Discrimination, Sexual Violence and Civil Liberties* (Oxford University Press, 1991). These are just two examples of studies that are difficult to refute. Others include work by Marshall and Check in Canada (see Zillman and Bryant, *op cit*).

11. *Pornography: Impacts and Influences* Cumberbatch and Howitt; Home Office (1990).

12. Their story is movingly told in two books: Ron Sims, *Flying Free: An Escape from Satan's Strongholds*; and Maureen Sims, *Looking for Love: A Life Transformed* (both Marshalls).

13. 'Report of the Committee on Obscenity and Film Censorship', HMSO 1979. (Proposal No 6 page 160.)

14. *Ibid*

15. 'Longitudinal content analysis of sexual violence in the bestselling erotica magazines', *Journal of Sex Research*, no 16 1980, pp 226-237.